THE 85 WAYS
TO TIE A TIE

THE 85 WAYS TO TIE A TIE

The Science and Aesthetics of Tie Knots

THOMAS FINK AND YONG MAO

FOURTH ESTATE • *London*

First published in Great Britain in 1999 by
Fourth Estate Limited
6 Salem Road
London W2 4BU
www.4thestate.co.uk

A catalogue record for this book is available from the British Library.

ISBN 1-84115-249-8

Text design by Robert Updegraff
Typeset by Robert Updegraff and Type Technique
Colour separations by Articolor, Verona
Printed in Great Britain by
Bath Press, Bath

CONTENTS

Acknowledgements

We gratefully acknowledge discussion with and advice from James Alexander, John Casey, Mike Cates, Clare Devlin, Robert Farr, Jonathan Harrison, Elizabeth Howard, Luke Howard, Andrew Mott, Barbara Ravelhofer, Ben Schott, Marzena Szymanska, Christian Waite, Mark Warner and Alex Wilson.

We also thank our editor Clive Priddle, designer Robert Updegraff and photographer Ben Schott, whose efforts improved this book immeasurably.

Ties were generously supplied by Gieves and Hawkes, Tie Rack and Austin Reed. Shirts and ties were provided by T. M. Lewin, to whom we are especially grateful.

Preface

'No one accustomed to mix with the higher classes of society will be at all inclined to dispute the advantages arising from a genteel appearance; it therefore becomes necessary that the means of acquiring this distinction should be clearly demonstrated. An attentive perusal of the following pages will conduce to this desired effect,' began the 1828 book *The Art of Tying the Cravat*. The treatise was published throughout Europe and in America in eleven editions. Apparently, the importance of a carefully arranged neckcloth began well before the modern tie was adopted.

The cravat disappeared and the long tie replaced it during the second half of the nineteenth century. The earliest tie knot, the four-in-hand, originated in England in the 1850s alongside the tie itself. The Duke of Windsor has been credited with introducing what is now known as the Windsor knot, whence its smaller derivative, the half-Windsor, is thought to have evolved. More recently, in 1989, the Pratt knot was revealed in broadsheets across the world, the first new knot to appear in 50 years.

The discovery of a new tie knot, evidently, is a rare event. We learnt of the Pratt in 1997. It seemed that there must be others. Rather than wait another half-century for the next knot, we considered a more formal approach.

If, as Le Blanc suggested, tying a cravat is an art, we found that tying a tie is a science. Tie knots, we realised, are equivalent to persistent random walks on a triangular lattice. (Our day job as theoretical physicists might have had something to do with it.) Some weeks later we had derived all of the 85 tie knots that can be tied with a conventional tie. We employed aesthetic conditions – expressed as mathematical constraints – to recover the four knots in widespread use and predict nine more aesthetic ones.

All of the knots are included in this book, though it is not simply meant to instruct. Nor does it attempt to describe the tie itself, such as its colour, pattern and shape. It concerns how the tie is arranged, and this has, throughout the last three centuries, invariably involved a knot. The plain cravats of the British Regency inspired a variety of styles to express what costly fabric had before. The choice and execution of the knot has, ever since, been of prime importance to a 'genteel appearance'.

The endpages show a 1926 photograph of the Fellows and students of the Cavendish Laboratory of Physics, where the authors work today. The tie had, by then, become ubiquitous, eclipsing its contemporaries the bow tie and Ascot. The knot was, inevitably, a four-in-hand. J. J. Thomson and Ernest Rutherford, who wear their knots with stiff collars, discovered the electron and nucleus. The young Robert Oppenheimer (second from the right, second row) later led the development of the first atomic bomb, known as the Manhattan project.

Seventy years later, the tie is worn by civilised men throughout the world. The tie's silk reflects light, in contrast to the dark cloth of the plain suit. It remains the central point of a man's costume. Choosing an appropriate knot, the essential personal touch, has never been easier.

Thomas Fink
Gonville and Caius College

Yong Mao
St. John's College

Cambridge, July 1999

CHAPTER ONE

A BRIEF HISTORY OF TIE KNOTS

If we, the Brits, cannot claim to have invented the modern
tie, no other nation can either. We do not have to trace…
its origins from the satin or velvet ribbon which held in
place the lace jabot, to the loose neckcloth named after the
battle of Steenkerk (3 August 1692), to Lord Guildford's
lawn, to Beau Brummell's cravats, to Comte d'Orsay's
pale-blue satin, to the sober black of Mr. Casaubon and all
the Victorian gentry. The cravat, of course, disappeared
with the frock and morning tail coat. The tie, as we know,
came to stay with the lounge suit.

Sir Hardy Amies
The Englishman's Suit

Antiquitie

Evidence of the earliest known knotted neckcloth lies in the tomb of China's first emperor, Qin Shih-huang-di (259–221 BC). In an elaborate underground mausoleum, an army of 7,500 sculptured terracotta soldiers sports knotted neckerchiefs. The discovery of the scarved army in 1974 was remarkable since not a single neckcloth could be found again in the subsequent numerous Chinese paintings and statues up to the seventeenth century, when European style began to be influential.

It had long been believed that Roman soldiers were the first to wear neckcloths. The marble Column of Trajan, erected in Rome by Emperor Traianus in AD 113, portrays some 2,500 carved figures, many depicted with neckcloths. Among the ancient neckerchiefs are ties apparently knotted in bows and early versions of what would, seventeen centuries later, become the standard knot for long ties: the four-in-hand. The pseudonymous book *The Art of Tying the Cravat* (1828) explained that the ancients 'defended [the throat] from the cold by means of a woollen or silken cloth, called in Rome *focalium*, a term which is evidently derived from *fauces* (the throat)'. But the treatise goes on to assert that a Roman considered it undignified to cover his throat except 'by hand, or occasionally wrapping the toga around it'. Indeed, Horace relates that neckcloths were thought to connote effeminacy and poor health. Perhaps this helps explain why neckwear is rarely found on Roman civilians and is instead restricted to military contexts where men had to endure harsh weather.

Apart from cases of necessity, ancient necks were largely undecorated, and this sobriety continued throughout the first 15 centuries AD.

A Chinese terracotta soldier displays the first knotted neckcloth.

Then, without warning but in stages, the neck became the focus of sartorial attention. In England the plain shirt collar, tied together with string, grew into a small frill under Henry VIII, eventually forming a ruff. The ruffs grew bigger and more lavish, but were suddenly decapitated with their royal patron Charles I with the defeat of the Royalists in the English Civil War. Not until the resurrection of the monarchy in 1660 did knotted neckcloths appear.

Croats in Cravats

It is commonly believed that the cravat, the modern tie's direct ancestor, originated during the Thirty Years' War (1618–1648). In his campaign against the Habsburg empire, King Louis XIII of France enlisted a regiment of Croatian cavalry. These mercenaries wore knotted neckcloths, and the new style was soon adopted by the French soldiers fighting alongside them. The cravat, as it came to be known, was ornamental but practical. Unlike the ruff collars in use at the time, which had to be laundered, starched and pressed, the new cravats required little maintenance and allowed freedom of movement.

The fashion was soon brought home to France, where it was adopted by dandies and members of the court. With the restoration of the English monarchy, Charles II returned to England to reclaim his throne after nine years in exile at the French court of Louis XIV. With him he brought the cravat which, within a decade, had become a familiar style in England and the American colonies.

*Charles II and the cravat he brought from
France to England on his restoration.*

The *Oxford English Dictionary* maintains that 'cravat' was derived from Croat, but evidence suggests otherwise: the word was used in France in the fourteenth century and Italy in the sixteenth century. The French writer Eustache Deschamps (c. 1340–1407), for instance, used the phrase *faites restraindre sa cravate* (pull his cravat tighter) in one of his ballads. Nonetheless, while the origin of the word may be unclear, there is little doubt that the modern cravat evolved from the mercenaries' neckwear.

These early cravats comprised a strip of fabric, made either of costly lace, or of muslin or cambric bordered with lace on both ends. They were wrapped once or twice around the neck and knotted or fastened in the front, leaving the two ends hanging freely. In the *Academy of Armoury and Blazon* (1688), Randle Holme described them as 'nothing else but a long Towel put about the Collar, and so tyed before with a Bow Knott'. The bow was in fact one of several knots used to tie cravats; the neckcloths were also tied with a slip knot or held together with a piece of ribbon. 'This procedure is easy to describe but not so easy to execute; a certain dexterity was required to achieve a satisfactory result,' writes François Chaille in *The Book of Ties*. The subtlety of arrangement was not a result of a complicated knot; inspection reveals that the slip knot was nothing more than a half-hitch, which is no more difficult to tie than the basic four-in-hand used today.

By the end of the seventeenth century, the cravat had become firmly established as a necessary accessory throughout Europe and the American colonies. Chaille suggests that the marked increase in the use of cravats may have resulted in part from a generally colder climate

17

between 1645 and 1715. The so-called 'Little Ice Age' was thought to be caused by a drop in solar activity known as the 'Maunder minimum', after the astrophysicist Edward Maunder. Given the ancient use of the knotted neckcloth as a practical garment, this is not implausible.

A new and unusual manner of tying the cravat, said to have originated at the Battle of Steenkerk in Flanders 1692, was adopted by the English in the 1690s. The Steenkerk, as it became known, consisted of a long, scarf-like cravat with ends of fringe or lace. It was loosely knotted and its ends were twisted together, with one of them placed through a buttonhole on the left side of the jacket. The style quickly gained popularity: 'I hope your Lordship is pleas'd with your Steenkerk,' wrote the playwright Sir John Vanbrugh in *The Relapse* in 1697. 'In love with it, stab my vitals!' The Steenkerk remained fashionable in Europe until the 1720s, but continued to be popular in America throughout most of the eighteenth century.

Into the Stocks

A markedly less flamboyant alternative, the stock was introduced – like the cravat – as military costume for foot soldiers in France and Germany in the beginning of the eighteenth century. It was initially adopted by young men who were keen to display their allegiance, real or implied, to the military. The stock soon became commonplace and remained fashionable throughout the last three-quarters of the eighteenth century.

The stock was initially a piece of white muslin folded into a narrow band, wound once or twice around the neck and pinned behind. As its popularity increased, the neckcloth was embellished,

William of Orange sports a Steenkerk, c. 1692.

comprising a whale-bone, pasteboard or leather stiffener covered by black or white material worn high around the neck. Because stocks lacked the loose ends of the cravat and did not cover the shirt front, they were sometimes accompanied by the jabot, a piece of white lace attached to the front of the stock. Particularly elegant was the *solitaire*, in which the black ribbon used to tie back the hair was brought to the front and tied in a bow, contrasting with the white stock worn underneath.

A white stock with jabot, worn by the French diplomat de Vergennes.

Unlike the cravat which preceded it, the stock was convenient. It was fastened behind the neck rather than tied in front, requiring little preparation and no maintenance. This, unfortunately, was offset by a loss of comfort. 'Invention has been racked to diversify it as much as possible; and, as appearance alone was consulted, each stage has rendered it more injurious; it has been transformed into a collar as hard as iron, by the insertion of a slip of wood,' observed *The Art of Tying the Cravat.*

When the Prince Regent ascended the throne as George IV in 1820, his preference for a black velvet stock with satin bow revived interest in the neckcloth which had long seemed to have reached its peak. The white stock 'was driven from all decent society by Geo. IV... and the black became the universal wear. William IV attempted to revive the white but scarcely succeeded,' observed the *Gentleman's Magazine of*

The bagwig and solitaire, *in a scene from Hogarth's* The Rake's Progress.

Fashion in 1838. The black stock, which remained popular until the 1850s, bore little resemblance to the high white collar which had preceded it. It was wrapped twice around the neck, this time with the ends meeting in front and tied there in a bow knot.

Macaronis and Incroyables

During the 1760s a group of young society men, inspired by the *mignon* style of the Continent and especially Italy, adopted a fashion of extravagance and excess. The Macaronis, as they soon came to be called, indulged in large perukes (powdered wigs), lavish embroidery, jewels and, not least, white cravats tied in enormous bows. 'Such a figure, essenced and perfumed, with a bunch of lace sticking out under its chin, puzzles the common passenger to determine the thing's sex,' deplored *Town and Country Magazine* in 1772.

The excessive style did not make its way to the American colonies. While innovations in American fashion followed Europe and especially England, they were sufficiently delayed and attenuated to produce only comparatively modest practices. America's Puritan founders encouraged little sympathy for elaborate dress, much less the Baroque ornamentation preferred by the Macaronis. This sobriety of fashion was expressed by the condescending song 'Yankee Doodle Dandy', written by a British soldier during the War of Independence and naively adopted by Americans:

> Yankee Doodle went to town,
> A-riding on a pony,
> Stuck a feather in his hat
> And called it Macaroni!

Beginning in the 1770s, Anglomania overtook France, and men strove to dress *à l'anglaise* despite a 20-year war between the two countries. The extravagance of the Macaronis was displayed in

After their grand tours of Italy, Macaronis indulged in extravagant dress and exaggerated bows.

France by the *Incroyables*, or Unbelievables. Excess was again the principal sin, this time seen in their exaggerated shoulders, wide lapels and large cravats. The eccentric neckwear required many yards of material, wound around the neck some ten times. The bow was not crucial but the cravat 'was increased to an almost incredible size', observed *The Art of Tying the Cravat*. Not surprisingly, the *Incroyables* 'were com-

The extraordinary Incroyables: *wide lapels, matched by big cravats.*

pelled to look straight before them, as the head could only be turned by general consent of all the members'.

In part due to the fashion of the Macaronis, cravats had made a revival by the 1780s, considerably evolved from the early fine articles embellished with lace. The new neckcloths consisted of large, square pieces of muslin or linen folded along the diagonal into a strip. They were often tied with an overhand knot or bow, albeit of more sensible proportions than those preferred by the Macaronis. Notably, the splendid lace of the early cravats began to disappear; what was once conveyed by expensive fabric increasingly had to be expressed by its aesthetic arrangement.

By George

The beginning of the nineteenth century marked the inception of a new sartorial philosophy. Contrary to popular understanding, dandyism was completely opposed to the flamboyant, studied style of the Macaronis and the *Incroyables*; unlike their predecessors, dandies sought perfection through simplicity rather than extravagance. Indeed, 'whatever else it was, [dandyism] was the *repudiation of fine feathers*', explains James Laver in *Dandies* (1968).

Its chief proponent was George Bryan Brummell (1778–1840). Beau Brummell, as he came to be known, was neither well-born nor rich, and by no means an aristocrat. Nevertheless, through determination, wit and impeccable dress, he reached the pinnacle of English society, befriended by – and eclipsing as an arbiter of good taste – the Prince of Wales, later George IV. For the first time, it was not simply what a man wore but how he wore it that made or broke his reputation as a gentleman. 'Brummell saw

Tying the perfect cravat: an English dandy in 1838.

instinctively that the day of aristocracy was over and that the day of gentility had arrived,' observes Laver.

He certainly spent hours at his toilette, but his aim was to appear inconspicuous. 'If John Bull turns round to look after you, you are not well dressed; but either too stiff, too tight, or too fashionable,' Brummell remarked. The Earl of Chesterfield expressed similar sentiment in a letter to his son. 'Take great care always to be dressed like the reasonable people of your own age, in the place where you are; whose dress is never spoken of one way or another as either too negligent or too much studied.'

Brummell's costume consisted of a close-fitting blue tailcoat, a buff waistcoat with matching pantaloons tucked into glossy black knee boots, and an immaculate white cravat, lightly starched the better to retain its desired shape – 'nothing more, nothing less. The clothes should be sombre, form-fitting but not restricting, severely plain and indubitably masculine,' writes Sarah Gibbings in *The Tie*. This ideal was to prove lastingly influential; Brummell's dress has prescribed the main lines of male fashion throughout Europe and America ever since. 'The best dressed man is the one who attracts the least attention,' Douglas Fairbanks Jr. remarked 100 years later.

By the time of Brummell's later financial ruin and exile into France, conspicuous inconspicuousness had become the accepted model for men's dress. A gentleman was to appear understated. Only in his cravat, which was usually white and invariably plain, could he display his individuality. The knot was everything. The vital role of the arrangement of neckwear was firmly established once and for all.

George Bryan 'Beau' Brummell led the renunciation of extravagance in men's dress.

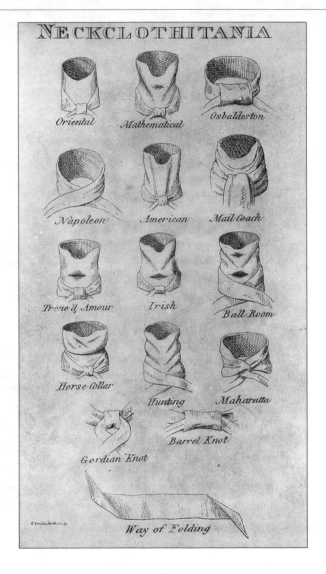

Cravatmania

Alongside, and as a result of, the dandyism of the period, cravats were approaching the height of their popularity. As men's dress became more discreet, the 'set of the cravat' was elevated to a letter of introduction. There soon emerged a myriad of ways to tie what was otherwise an unexpressive garment.

More than one book was written to guide men through the increasingly formidable routine. *Neckclothitania; or, Tietania*, one of the first (1818), details 12 popular styles. The anonymous author sought to leave 'a clear and distinct line drawn between *l'homme comme il faut* [a proper gentleman], and *la canaille* [a cad]' by providing the aspiring gentleman with the means of becoming one – at least as regards his neck tie.

L'Art de se mettre la cravate appeared in Paris in 1827 under the pseudonym Baron Émile de l'Empesé (literally translated Baron of Starch). That same year, a similar volume was published in Italy by 'conte della Salda', or Count Starch, and in England as *The Art of Tying the Cravat* by H. Le Blanc. As it was issued by Honoré de Balzac's printer, many people have suspected that the international seller was written by the young author. It is now believed that the book was in fact written by Émile-Marc de Saint-Hilaire, though Balzac was indeed responsible for the preface. In either event, the book was published in eleven editions and was immensely successful throughout Europe.

The treatise describes 32 ways of tying a cravat, such as the *Cravate à l'Americaine, Cravate à l'Orientale, Cravate Collier de Chavale* and *Cravate à la Byron*. More extensive than *Neckclothitania*, it was also written with a sense of irony which might have confused those most in need of its advice. The *Cravate Mathématique* requires 'a combination of symmetry and regularity – the style is grave and severe, and the slightest wrinkle is prohibited. The ends should be geometrically correct, and must bear examination even by the aid of a compass.' The name of the *Cravate Sentimentale*, it warned, 'is sufficient to explain that it is not alike suitable to all faces'. Rest assured that 'if your physiognomy does not inspire sensations of love and passion, and you should adopt the *Cravate Sentimentale*, you will be a fair butt for the shafts of ridicule, which (with no unsparing hand) will be showered upon you on all sides.'

Cravatmania peaked with the publication of *L'Art de la toilette* in 1830, detailing 72 ways of tying the cravat. The increasing numbers of knots outlined by this and the preceding treatises were, however, misleading. Invariably, the different styles involved variations on overhand, square and bow knots. The details of arrangement often received as much attention as the knots themselves. *Neckclothitania* observed that the 'American Tie differs little from the Mathematical, except that the collateral indentures do not extend so near to the ear, and that there is no horizontal or middle crease in it.' Confusing the two would be inexcusable.

From Beau to Bow

The prevailing style of early Victorian dress required increasingly high-buttoned jackets, which could no longer accommodate the large, variously knotted cravats. Moreover, 'more and more men obliged to wear cravats found that, unlike dandies and followers of the Baron de l'Empesé, they could not afford to spend considerable amounts of time knotting them every morning. Members of the new work-force required neckwear which was easy to put on, comfortable, and sturdy enough to survive an exhausting work day,' explains Chaille. 'The need for a practical tie — one that would neither impede movement nor come undone — was also felt by men in the leisure class who were beginning to lead more active lives.' The result was the emergence of a number of new styles of neckwear, each having evolved in a different direction from the cravat. Towards the end of the nineteenth century the variety was at its greatest, though three primary forms could be distinguished: the bow tie, the Ascot and the four-in-hand or long tie.

The bow in its earliest form was used to tie the early lace cravats of the seventeenth century, and it remained more or less fashionable during the next 300 years. Indeed, the modern bow tie is already discernible in a number of the styles of the Regency cravats. As the popularity of the bow increased, its size diminished, and by the end of the nineteenth century two familiar varieties were commonplace:

James Clerk Maxwell, Cavendish professor of physics 1871–1879.

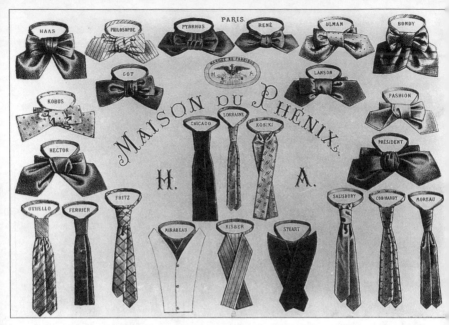

Maison du Phénix: a French catalogue from 1863 showing the evolution of the cravat.

the butterfly and the batswing. Both have since remained in use, though the butterfly is the more common of the two. Today a black silk bow tie is worn with a dinner jacket (no coloured varieties, please) and a stiff white tie with evening tails. 'This and the stiff wing collar are the direct descendants of Beau Brummell's starched cravats. He had trouble tying these. How could the rising middle classes cope?... I cannot blame men for buying "made-up" ties, sin though it is to wear one,' writes Hardy Amies in *The Englishman's Suit*.

The genealogy of the Ascot, if less ancient than the bow tie, is no less impressive. It is essentially identical to the Gordian cravat of the early nineteenth century, with its blades wider and neck band narrower. Both were tied in a square or Gordian knot (from which the cravat took its name) with the loose ends brought one over the other before being fixed with a pin. The Ascot became popular in the 1880s, worn by the upper-middle classes out of doors and at the Royal Ascot race, from which the neckcloth took its name. In England it remains commonplace at weddings and the annual horse race.

It is curious that the bow tie and the Ascot – requiring two of the most elementary knots known – are most likely to be purchased ready tied. It is perhaps reassuring (though by no means mitigating) that early contemporaries of the neckwear did not find them straightforward either. 'They may appear rather complicated, but I have followed out each move in front of a glass, and if you do the same, you won't find any difficulty in tying your ties in the future,' instructs the 'Major', the pseudonymous author of the 1900 guide to dress *Clothes and the Man*.

The Four-in-hand

No one knows precisely when the four-in-hand tie was first used, or by whom, although it was initially fashionable in England in the 1850s as young men's sporting attire The four-in-hand quickly gained popularity and the new style was widespread within a decade.

Although their fundamental attributes have not changed, four-in-hand ties of the late nineteenth century did not closely resemble those used today. The early ties were simple, rectangular strips of material with identical square ends. Because they were cut along the straight rather than the bias and occasionally lined with coarse material, the primitive ties were inelastic and had to be folded as much as tied into loose knots. The ends hung no lower than the sternum, as they only had to reach the waistcoats commonly worn at the time. 'When tied the centre knot presented a horizontal border along the top and bottom. The two ends [were] nearly the same width and cut square; and hanging one over the other down the midline,' so C. W. and P. Cunnington describe it in the *Handbook of English Costume in the 19th Century.*

At the end of the eighteenth century, 'four-in-hand' was used to describe a carriage with four horses driven by one person. Later it was the name of a (now defunct) London gentlemen's club. Some

'A well-tied tie is the first serious step in life' – Oscar Wilde, 1891.

Newnham College Hockey XI, 1897.

report that the carriage drivers tied their scarves in the manner of the four-in-hand; others that the knot was used in four-in-hand reins. More likely, members of the Four-in-Hand Club wore their neckcloths according to the new style and the club's name persisted.

The first knot with which four-in-hand ties were tied appeared with the advent of the tie itself. At the time, the tie and the knot were inseparable, and 'four-in-hand' was used to describe both. Today, owing to its exclusivity, the four-in-hand tie has been abbreviated to 'tie' or 'long tie', and 'four-in-hand' is used to designate one of a number of knots. But until the 1930s, it appears that only the four-in-hand knot was in widespread use.

In the early 1900s the tie knot itself was under threat from the emerging ready-made tie industry. Then, as now, wearing a ready-made was an act of sartorial terrorism. 'Of course no gentleman ever does wear a made-up tie... I consider it part of the duty of every father to tell his son this on leaving school,' admonishes the 'Major'. 'The young man who always tries to get a tie of the same material and colour as *her* dress doesn't make such a fool of himself as the young man who goes to a shop and lays in a stock of ready-made ties.' Fortunately, ready-made ties are today no more common than the matching bow.

The rapidly increasing popularity of the four-in-hand tie can partly be attributed to the demise of the stiff single collar in favour of the soft turned-down collar towards the end of the nineteenth century. While bow ties and Ascots best suited stiff collars, the small opening of the turned-down collar framed the four-in-hand knot superbly. The staff and students of the Cavendish Laboratory in Cambridge (1926) are pictured in the endpages of this book. The four-in-hand tie and knot are ubiquitous and turned-down collars are widespread. Only professors J. J. Thomson and Ernest Rutherford wear their four-in-hands with stiff collars.

Despite the popularity of the four-in-hand tie, it was neither easy nor practical to tie the unwieldy fabric into a satisfactory knot. Apart from allowing a limited range of styles, the knot often loosened, 'and away [went] your tie halfway down your shirt front'. By 1900 an enormous variety of pins and clips were available to ensure that the tie stayed tied and secured to the shirt, and with them instructions on their use. 'If you are wearing a black tie, or a black tie with a white pattern or a red pattern, nothing beats a plain single pearl,' advises the 'Major'.

The tie's shortcomings, which had everything to do with its construction, were first resolved by the New Yorker Jesse Langsdorf in 1926. He introduced ties cut on the bias, or diagonal, allowing the tie to stretch along its length, and constructed them from three separate segments of material. The resulting ties were elastic and resilient and fell straight from the knot without twisting. With this small but revolutionary innovation the modern tie was born.

Ernest Rutherford, discoverer of the nucleus, wears a four-in-hand, c. 1915.

The shape of the tie, if not its design, did continue to change. As waistcoats became less fashionable, ties increased in length to fill the larger space left by the lapels of the jacket. Today, at the close of the century, the tie just reaches the waist of the trousers. But as 350 years of tradition have reminded us, the tie is, after all, neckwear. It is better to wear it too short than too long. The width of the tie has been endowed with as much significance as the size of the cravat two centuries before. The exaggerated kipper ties popular in the 1970s saw much the same reaction as the excessive bows and cravats of the Macaronis and *Incroyables* that preceded them. The width of the tie has in this century fluctuated between two and five inches, usually in synchrony with the width of jacket lapels. The natural width of a tie, which reflects the unexaggerated proportions of a man's suit, is three to three and a half inches. Many of the men's shops in London's Jermyn Street, like Hackett, have continued to produce their entire stocks in these sizes.

The Windsor, Not

It was not until after the tie's transformation by Langsdorf that its potential diversity of arrangements began to be realised. Because it was cut along the bias, the tie allowed more discreet knots, capable of taking on a variety of shapes. At the same time, the tie had reached unprecedented popularity and men's dress was at its most elegant this century. Inevitably, the long-standing domination of the four-in-hand knot finally came to an end.

Perhaps the most notable of all new knots, the Windsor became popular in the mid-1930s. The Prince of Wales, later King Edward VIII and later still the Duke of Windsor, had an immense impact on the fashion of his day. His affair with the American divorcée Wallis Simpson brought the already influential Prince to the foreground of American attention. He had a preference for large knots and spread collars in which to accommodate them, and the public followed his lead.

While the Duke of Windsor certainly played a role in popularising the large knot bearing his name, it is well established that he did not invent it. More surprisingly, the Duke did not use the Windsor knot, but rather the four-in-hand tied in specially designed thick ties. 'That may be the origin of the myth of the Windsor knot which the Duke does *not* wear,' reported *Vogue* in 1967. The end result was a knot which possessed a bulk that others could achieve only with a larger knot.

Less is known about the half-Windsor, though we can be certain it was not uncommon by the 1950s. Apart from its name, there is little to suggest that it is a derivative of the Windsor knot that supposedly preceded it. Moreover, its etymology cannot be strictly true; it is three-quarters the size of the Windsor and not, as its name suggests, half. Nevertheless, the name persisted and the knot attracted a following that remains strong today.

The Second World War marked the end of British sartorial dominance, at least with respect to ties, and American influence gained momentum. The popularity of the conservative, understated ties fashionable before the war – expressing what *Esquire* called an 'object lesson in restraint' – ended with it. They were succeeded by 'bold look' ties, displaying an unprecedented diversity of colour and pattern and reflecting the optimism of the time. The acceptance of whimsy in men's neckwear has continued to a greater or lesser extent ever since.

It was not until the 1980s, when the often prophesied demise of the tie proved false and styles became less flamboyant, that the arrangement of the tie, rather than its pattern, again received significant attention. In 1989, with the four-in-hand, Windsor and half-Windsor dominant, the Pratt knot was revealed in the pages of broadsheets across the world. It was invented by the American Jerry Pratt, who had been wearing the knot unwittingly for decades before its rise to popularity.

What a tie would do for a man in 1951.

Nearly 170 years after the publication of *Neckclothitania*, the Italians Davide Mosconi and Riccardo Villarosa wrote the guide to neck-tie knots, *Getting Knotted* (1985), later republished as *The Book of Ties*. Unlike its predecessors, the book describes how to tie all forms of neckwear. It details 34 ways to wear a four-in-hand tie, although these are in fact variations on some nine principal knots shown in its endpages. The redundancy stems from a loose definition of 'knot': a four-in-hand in a wide tie and a narrow tie can produce an altogether different appearance, but the conformation in which both are arranged is identical.

How many distinct knots can be tied with a tie? In the case of the cravat, the number of styles outlined during the first half of the nineteenth century increased from 12 to 32 to 72. It will therefore come as no surprise that the number of tie knots is far greater than most people realise.

Now that sartorial manners have returned and men once again give due attention to the arrangement of their neckcloths, science offers not only a means of calculating all possible knots but also the conditions under which any are aesthetically pleasing. Linking together 350 years of tradition and mathematical analysis will produce the science and aesthetics of tie knots.

First Cock Sparrow. "WHAT A MIWACKULOUS TYE, FWANK. HOW THE DOOSE DO YOU MANAGE IT?"

Second Cock Sparrow. "YAS. I FANCY IT IS RATHER GRAND; BUT THEN, YOU SEE, I GIVE THE WHOLE OF MY MIND TO IT!"

CHAPTER TWO

TOPOLOGY,
KNOTS AND TIES

Knotting ought to be reckoned, in the scale of
insignificance, next to mere idleness.

Dr. Samuel Johnson
Dictionary, 1755

Nodus Operandi

Knots play a more fundamental role in the natural world than their sartorial prominence might suggest. DNA is known to take on knotted conformations, for instance when it receives a crossover in recombination; this in turn affects its properties. Less intuitively, knots in ten dimensions may play a role in string theory, which attempts to reconcile general relativity with quantum mechanics. In the minds of most people, however, knots are purely practical, and this will be our starting point.

The word 'knot', in its usual sense, 'applies to all complications in cordage, except accidental ones, such as snarls and kinks, and complications adapted for storage, such as coils, hanks, skeins, balls, *etc.*', according to *The Ashley Book of Knots*. In practice, this broad definition is divided into three principal categories: bends, hitches and knots. A bend unites two ropes, a hitch makes fast a rope to another object and a knot is any conformation tied in the rope itself.

The most familiar and frequently used knots are the most elementary. The simplest knot is the overhand (Figure 1) which, when tied around an object, is called a half-hitch. The square or reef knot is perhaps the most common, often confused with the similar but essentially useless granny knot. The bow is tied like the square knot, the only difference being that the second half is made with both ends of the rope doubled back. The slip knot is (confusingly) another type of hitch, more secure than the half-hitch, with the buntline more dependable yet.

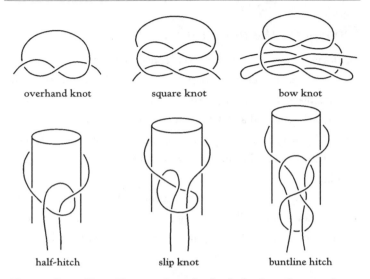

| overhand knot | square knot | bow knot |
| half-hitch | slip knot | buntline hitch |

Figure 1 *Practical knots. The seemingly rare buntline hitch, when tied in a tie, is better known as the four-in-hand.*

Surprisingly, most of the knots used to tie neckcloths, outlined in Chapter 1, are among the elementary knots shown in Figure 1. The early lace cravats were tied in a half-hitch or slip knot. Many of the Regency cravats, such as the Gordian, required a square knot, as did the later popular Ascot. Black stocks and bow ties employed a bow knot and the long tie was, until the early twentieth century, exclusively tied in a buntline hitch, better known as the four-in-hand.

Men have used elementary knots to fasten their neckcloths for centuries. More complicated knots exist, though it is not clear which are suitable for ties. To understand tie knots in the context of knots, we first consider some basic concepts in topology.

Topology – the doughnut in the teacup

Topology is a branch of geometry concerned with properties of shapes that do not change upon stretching and contracting, as if they are made of rubber. A small ball and a big ball are topologically identical, and a globe is a topological representation of our planet. Likewise, in the eyes of a topologist, an apple and a banana are equivalent, since the surface of one can be stretched into that of the other.

Some shapes cannot be deformed into others, no matter how stretchy they are. A ball for instance cannot assume the shape of a doughnut, or torus, without a puncture – a doughnut has a hole and

Figure 2 *The objects above can be continuously deformed into the objects below, though not always in three dimensions; two linked rings can unlink only in four or more dimensions.*

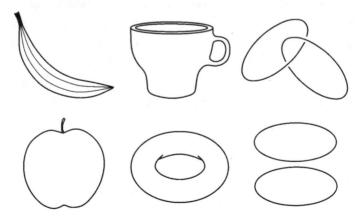

46

a ball does not. A teacup, however, can take on the shape of a doughnut, by shrinking the cup and inflating the handle.

Topological equivalence between two shapes requires that one can be continuously deformed into the other without cutting or pasting, or introducing or removing holes. This definition, when pursued mathematically, can lead to some very strange places indeed.

Two linked rings, for example, can be continuously manipulated into two unlinked rings without cutting either. The apparent impossibility of this result is an artefact of thinking in three dimensions: the rings can be unlinked in four or more dimensions only. The reasoning may be illustrated by considering an analogous example in a two-dimensional world. A beetle trying to escape from an island cannot manage simply by crawling (i.e., travelling on the two-dimensional surface of the earth), but succeeds by flying (using the additional third dimension). Similarly, with the control of a fourth dimension, say, time, we can make one ring time-travel forwards so that the two rings exist at different instances. Either of the rings can then be moved in space without passing through the other; the puzzle is solved.

The example of linked rings serves as a warning against the use of intuition. Indeed, a string cannot be knotted in four (or more) dimensions; like the link between the rings, all entanglements vanish. In our pursuit of tie knots, however, we happily consider only three-dimensional space.

Knot Theory

The search for a deeper understanding of knots started with the physicist Lord Kelvin. He was a prominent researcher at a time when a theory of the atom was wanting. The stability and variety of atoms was known but not understood, and Lord Kelvin thought that they might have been made of different knots and vortices in the background ether (empty space was, at the time, heavily suspect). In an 1867 presentation to the Royal Society of Edinburgh, he concluded: 'Models of knotted and linked vortex atoms were presented to the Society, the infinite variety of which is more than sufficient to explain the allotropies and affinities of all known matter.' Apparently, he was inspired by the smoke rings of his physicist friend P. G. Tait, and soon became convinced that all matter was made up of knotty vortices not dissimilar to the variety of smoke rings he saw. Soon afterwards, Tait set to work enumerating the different possible knots in an effort to verify Kelvin's claim.

By 1877, Tait had enumerated all knots up to seven crossings. He had hoped that they would correlate with the elements in the periodic table. They didn't, and Lord Kelvin was mistaken, but knot theory was born nevertheless.

Over a century later, knot theory is now firmly established as a branch of mathematics in its own right. Although knots often arise naturally in a way familiar to everyone, they are unusually difficult to formulate and analyse. Referring to his own knot table, Tait readily admitted that 'there may still be some [knots] omitted, while others may be retained in more than one group'. The absence of exact methods was later evident when K. M. Perko discovered in 1974 that two knots – thought distinct for 90 years – were in fact identical. This air of uncertainty shows knot theory to be a particularly challenging field.

It is common to think of knots as complications in a piece of rope with two free ends, such as an overhand or square knot. But when mathematicians think about a knot, they prefer first to splice the loose ends together to 'keep in' the knottedness. In this way any piece of string adjoining itself carries a knot, and conversely any knot can be represented by such a string. Two knots are equivalent if one can be manipulated to look like the other, and are different otherwise.

The simplest knot is the ordinary loop shown in Figure 3, usually known as the unknot. It plays a role in knot theory similar to the number zero in the natural numbers (non-negative integers) under

Figure 3 *The knots above are identical to the unknot (top left) and the knots below are identical to the trefoil (bottom left).*

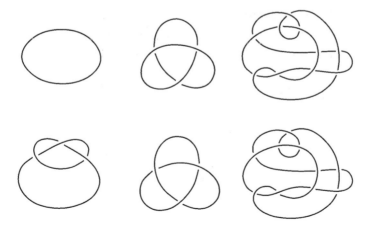

addition. The simplest *non-trivial* knot is the trefoil, which is identical to the overhand knot with its ends joined. Try as one might, the trefoil cannot be manipulated into the unknot.

Determining whether or not two knots are identical can, in practice, be very difficult, as Perko and Tait could have testified. To illustrate this point, in Figure 3 (centre) the unknot and the trefoil are drawn to look more similar: they differ only by a single crossing. When they are further complicated (right), it is not at all obvious which is which.

For all but the simplest knot, a drawing of a knot necessarily crosses itself. The minimum number of such intersections is known as the crossing index. The trefoil, for instance, can be drawn with three or more crossings, but not fewer. It is the only knot with a crossing index of three. Figure 4 illustrates knots with crossing indices four and five. The knot on the left is called the figure-eight knot. There are two distinct knots with five crossings, neither of which can be deformed into the other.

The crossing index is used by knot theorists to characterise a knot's topological complexity. The number of knots per index, in

Figure 4 *A knot of crossing index four, called the figure-eight knot (left). Two knots of crossing index five, neither of which can be manipulated into the other (right).*

Tait's words, 'grow[s] at a fearfully rapid rate', but to this day little is known about this series of numbers.

Tie Knot Theory

A tied tie is simply a knotted strip of fabric worn around the neck. Not surprisingly, ideas developed in knot theory may be used to study tie knots. As before, we imagine the two ends of the tie, once knotted, to be joined together. We now need a definition or mathematical description of a tie knot. This description must be complete and specific, distinguishing between all tie knots and ruling out tangles of fabric that are of no use to a gentleman.

The simplest answer, carried over from the previous section, is that a tie knot is any closed contour of tie, with two knots equivalent if one can be deformed into the other and distinct otherwise. However, as can be verified in practice, both the four-in-hand and the Windsor can then be manipulated into the trefoil, and the half-Windsor and the Pratt into the unknot. Apparently, this definition does not capture the full complexity of tie knots; we need a more sensitive classification.

The problem lies in the implicit constraints which tie knots must satisfy. While an ordinary knot can be untangled in any way so long as it is not cut, a tie knot is constrained to loop around the neck above and hang against the chest below. Accordingly, we introduce a link or peg at the top of the knot to represent the neck, and a second peg below to capture the constraint that the two ends may not be pulled through. This construction, shown in Figures 5 and 6, gives rise to a distinct class of knots called two-peg knots.

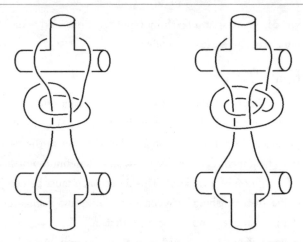

Figure 5 *The two-peg knot representation of the four-in-hand (left) and the half-Windsor (right). The top peg corresponds to the neck and the bottom peg constrains the two descending ends.*

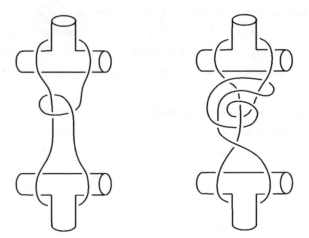

Figure 6 *Some two-peg knots are unsuitable for ties.*

The two-peg representation of the four-in-hand and the Windsor are now distinct in the sense that one cannot be deformed into the other. Indeed, every known tie knot corresponds to a unique two-peg knot. We thus have a model sufficiently detailed to describe all known tie knots. Unfortunately, it appears to include knots that are not suitable for ties (Figure 6). To establish a one-to-one representation, we must turn to a rather different approach. We consider how the knot is tied in practice.

Tie Knot Practice

Once a tie is placed around the neck, the wide (active) end is wrapped around the narrow (passive) end in such a way that the latter is free to slip through the resulting knot. We propose to enumerate the different ways to tie a tie by considering all possible manipulations of the active end.

A tie knot is begun by wrapping the active end to the left and either over or under the passive end, forming the three-spoke basis and dividing the space into right, centre and left (R, C, L) regions (Figure 7).

The knot is continued by winding the active end around the three-spoke basis. This process may be considered a sequence of half-turns from one region to another so that the direction of the active end alternates between out of the shirt ($\odot$) and into the shirt ($\otimes$) (Figure 8). These two symbols correspond to the head and tail of an arrow.

To complete a knot, the active end must be wrapped over the front, i.e., either $R\odot L\otimes$ or $L\odot R\otimes$, then underneath to the centre,

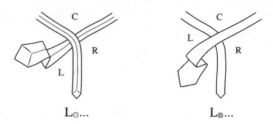

Figure 7 *The two ways of beginning a knot. For knots beginning with $L_\odot$, the tie must begin inside out. (This and all other figures are drawn in the frame of reference of a mirror image of the actual tie.)*

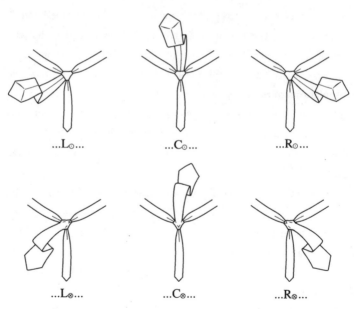

Figure 8 *The six moves with which a tie knot is tied. The move $L_\odot$, for instance, indicates the move which places the active end into the left region and directed out of the page.*

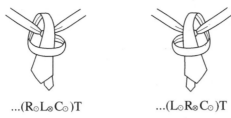

$...(R_\odot L_\otimes C_\odot)T$ $...(L_\odot R_\otimes C_\odot)T$

Figure 9 *The two ways of completing a knot. The active end is finally put through (denoted* T) *the front loop constructed by the last three moves.*

$C_\odot$, and finally through (denoted T but not considered a move) the front loop just made (Figure 9).

We can now define a tie knot as any sequence of moves chosen from the set $\{R_\odot, R_\otimes, C_\odot, C_\otimes, L_\odot, L_\otimes\}$, beginning with $L_\odot$ or $L_\otimes$ and ending with $R_\odot L_\otimes C_\odot T$ or $L_\odot R_\otimes C_\odot T$. The sequence is constrained so that no two consecutive moves indicate the same region (e.g., $R_\odot$ $R_\otimes$) or the same direction (e.g., $C_\odot L_\odot$). The four-in-hand, for instance, is indicated by the sequence $L_\otimes R_\odot L_\otimes C_\odot T$ (Figure 10).

Every tie knot corresponds to a distinct sequence and every valid sequence to a distinct knot suitable for ties. Finally, we have a satisfactory definition of tie knots.

If we regard the R, C and L moves as steps on a triangular lattice, each tie knot corresponds to a random walk. By pursuing this connection, we can use techniques in physics to classify tie knots according to their size and shape and quantify the number of knots in each class. Aesthetic constraints of symmetry and balance are then imposed. A summary of our results follows; details of the model can be found in the Appendix.

Figure 10 *The four-in-hand, represented by the sequence* L⊗R⊙L⊗C⊙T.

Size and Shape

The size of a tie knot corresponds to the number of moves, or half-turns, necessary to tie it. Additional moves increase knot size, although a small knot tied in a thick tie may resemble a big knot tied in a thin tie. Combining the initial and terminal subsequences generates the smallest knot possible; it consists of three moves and is given by the sequence L⊙R⊗C⊙T. In theory, there is no limit to how big a tie knot can be. Real ties, however, have finite length, usually between 52 and 58 inches. Accordingly, only knots that leave sufficient length to loop around the neck and through the knot are possible in practice. Though this depends on the weight of the tie, we exclude knots of ten moves or more. Summing the number of knots per size from three moves to nine (namely, 1, 1, 3, 5, 11, 21 and 43), the total number of possible tie knots is 85 (details of this and other calculations can be found in the Appendix).

The shape of the knot is determined by the number of right, centre and left moves necessary to tie it. In practice, a knot is judged by its width, and this is characterised by the number of centres. We use it to classify knots of equal size; knots with identical size and shape belong to the same class. A small fraction of centre moves forms a narrow knot, such as the four-in-hand, and a large centre fraction forms a broad knot, such as the Windsor.

The 85 knots comprise a total of 16 classes, namely (3,1), (4,1), (5,1), (5,2), (6,1), (6,2), (7,1), (7,2), (7,3), (8,1), (8,2), (8,3), (9,1), (9,2), (9,3) and (9,4), where the first entry is the number of moves and the second the number of centre moves. Classes (7,1), (8,1) and (9,1) do not contain knots sufficiently aesthetic to merit attention, leaving 13 principal knot classes.

Symmetry and Balance

The symmetry of a knot, which is the first aesthetic constraint, is employed to select for knots with a near equal number of left and right moves. It is defined as the difference between the two numbers, which we seek to minimise.

Whereas the number of centre moves and the symmetry indicate the move composition of a knot sequence, balance relates to the distribution of these moves; it corresponds to the extent to which the moves are well mixed. A well balanced knot is tightly bound and keeps its shape. We use it as the second aesthetic constraint.

The knots in each class are ordered according to symmetry and, in the event of a tie, by balance. The first knot in each principal class is defined as an aesthetic knot. In this way, our model duly predicts the four knots in widespread use and further introduces nine new aesthetic knots.

Duplicity and Ambiguity

The tie knots described in this book could equally well be tied beginning with $R\otimes$ and $R\odot$. (Left-handed men will have been doing this for some time.) Since a knot and its transpose are mirror images of each other, we do not duplicate them here and opt to restrict our discussion to knots starting from the left only.

Certain knot names are used indiscriminately to describe more than one knot sequence. These sequences differ by the transposition of one or more LR (or RL) pairs; for instance, $L\otimes R\odot C\otimes R\odot L\otimes C\odot T$ is also known as the half-Windsor, $L\otimes R\odot C\otimes L\odot R\otimes C\odot T$. This ambiguity primarily results from the absence of definitive definitions, although the transposition of the last LR group is favourable. It determines whether or not a sequence is self-releasing (see below) – a convenience some will find offsets any aesthetic loss.

Untying the Knot

A tie knot is most easily and most often untied by pulling the passive end out through the knot. This is bad for the tie but sometimes convenient for the wearer: the tie either straightens or retains a residual smaller knot. Interestingly, the complexity of the remaining knot does not depend on the length of the sequence from which it was generated. The Windsor, for instance, unties fully but the half-Windsor does not.

It turns out that knots ending with the terminal subsequence $R\odot L\otimes C\odot T$ untie fully, but knots ending with $L\odot R\otimes C\odot T$ lose this self-releasing property. Figure 11 illustrates the subtle topological

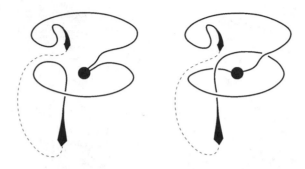

Figure 11 *The left diagram, with terminal subsequence R⊙L⊗C⊙T, is unknotted, while the right, with terminal subsequence L⊙R⊗C⊙T, forms a trefoil knot.*

difference between the two finishing subsequences. Once the passive end is removed, the pre-terminal sequence of moves resembles a ball of string with two loose ends. Pulling on the active end causes it to unravel. Accordingly, all moves collapse except for the terminal subsequence, which then determines whether the tie will self-release.

Science has provided us with 85 tie knots – theoretically. But the theory has to be put into practice. Of the 85 knots, 13 have survived our aesthetic tests and earned our recommendation. They are shown in detail, together with observations about their particular qualities and associations, in Chapter 3. The remainder, some of which have had a following during the twentieth century, are included for completeness. Theory, unfortunately, will not account for personal preference; you will have to try them for yourself.

CHAPTER THREE

THE 85 TIE KNOTS

A Cravatte is … [tied] with a Bow Knott; this is the
Original of all such Wearings; but now by the Art and
Inventions of the seamsters, there is so many new ways
of making them, that it would be a Task to name, much
more to describe them.

Randle Holme
Academy of Armoury and Blazon, 1688

Three-Move Knots

Knot 1 (Oriental)

One Centre

L∘R⊗C∘T

Although it is the most elementary tie knot possible, the Oriental is used infrequently in the West. In China it takes the place of its next-of-kin, the four-in-hand (2), as the first knot taught to school-boys. It has been variously known throughout the East and West as the simple knot, red knot and *petit noeud*.

The Oriental requires that the tie begin inside-out around the neck, which may explain its rarity. While the passive (narrow) end remains inside-out after completing the knot, the active (wide) end finishes outside-out. This results from first bringing the active end *under* the passive end rather than over (first move, opposite), and applies to all knots comprising an odd number of moves, or half-turns.

It is widely accepted that, until ties were cut on the bias or diagonal in the 1920s, the four-in-hand was the only knot in use. But the tie drawn on page 64, from *Pearsall's Illustrated Handbook for Knitting in Silks* (1904), casts doubt on the early exclusivity of the four-in-hand knot. Superficially, the knot appears to be a four-in-hand, but closer inspection reveals otherwise. Like the Oriental, the knot on page 64 leans towards the active end (in this case the blade coming from what would be the left of the neck). In contrast, a four-in-hand knot leans towards the passive end. Although it is difficult to differentiate between these two knots when worn, it is evident from the *Handbook* alone that the Oriental enjoyed some following early in the twentieth century.

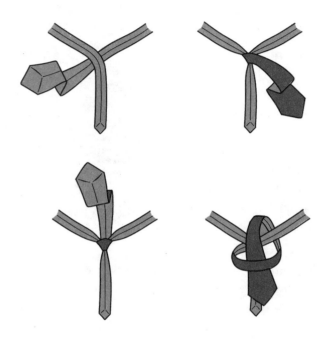

The Oriental has its shortcomings: without close attention it can end up awkwardly shaped and, because of its simple structure, it may loosen with time. Its primary advantage is its small size, which can prove indispensable for ties made of heavy fabric, such as woven, knitted or wool ties. With certain intransigent ties the authors use nothing else.

Small knots, such as the Oriental, four-in-hand (2) and Kelvin (3), use a short length of tie and may leave one or both ends too long. 'Though it may be acceptable in England, a

KNITTED SAILOR'S-KNOT TIE (NARROW), IN DOUBLE KNITTING, STRIPED OR PLAIN.

Materials :—If Plain, 1 oz. Ball Pearsall's "Extra Quality" or "Empress" Knitting Silk. If Striped, ½ oz. Ball in addition of the colour stripe desired. 2 Needles, No. 18.

(*This Tie is about 1¼ inches wide.*)

THE directions below are for horizontal stripes, but if the Tie is desired plain, the stripes can be omitted, *i.e.* the rows in colour B should be worked with colour A.

Cast on, in colour A, 30 stitches. Double knitting is worked as follows :—Silk in front, slip 1, silk back, knit 1. This is repeated throughout. Work 6 rows colour A, 1 row colour B, 2 rows A, 1 row B, 2 rows A, 1 row B. It must be remembered that in double knitting, a forward and backward row count as one. Work in these stripes for 18 inches. To decrease for the

N.B.—*The Instructions apply to Pearsall's Silks only.*

Pearsall's Illustrated Handbook for Knitting in Silks, 1904.

tie's length should not be seen falling below the waistband of your trousers. If your tie is too long, tuck the offending excess into your pants in the style of Fred Astaire or the Duke of Windsor. The bottom will get wrinkled, but if it's always worn this way, it can only offend your closet,' advises Alan Flusser in *Style and the Man*. Only if covered by a waistcoat. Instead, untie the tie and try again; once the front blade is the proper length, the passive end can, if necessary, be tucked between two buttons into the shirt.

CHARLIE CHAPLIN
(CHARLOT)

125

Four-Move Knots One Centre
Knot 2 (Four-in-hand) L⊗R⊙L⊗C⊙T

The four-in-hand is the best-known and most commonly used knot today. Because of its simplicity (and familiarity to fathers), learning how to tie the knot invariably forms a boy's rite of passage. Unfortunately, as men they rarely take the time to learn anything else.

The pedigree of the four-in-hand is impeccable. As the cravat of the British Regency gave way to more practical forms of neckwear, the long tie was adopted and along with it the four-in-hand knot. By the 1860s the style had become fashionable and both the tie and the knot have had a substantial following ever since.

The four-in-hand most likely derives its name from the nineteenth-century London gentlemen's club of the same name. Patrons of the Four-in-Hand Club adopted the long tie knotted in the new style and the club's name was soon used to describe it. As explained in Chapter 1, it has also been suggested that 'four-in-hand' derives from the four-in-hand carriage (drawn by a team of four horses driven by one man) in use at the time. Some argue that the knot was used in tying the reins of the horses, others that the drivers tied their scarves in the same way. In any event, the word does not, as some will have concluded, describe the four moves needed to tie it.

The four-in-hand is a slender, tapered knot, which 'should not be overly triangular: a dash of asymmetry adds a salutary touch of poetry,' advises François Chaille in *The Book of Ties*. Despite its

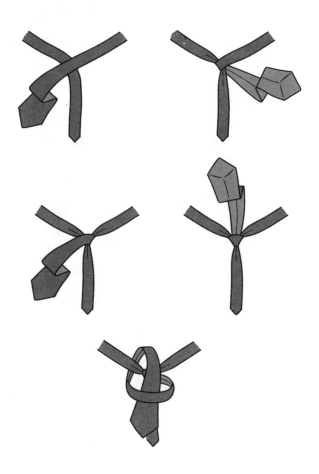

usually being adopted out of negligence, some men, like Alan Flusser, admire the four-in-hand in its own right. 'It is the smallest and most precise of knots, and it has been the staple of the natural-shouldered, British-American style of dress ... for the past fifty years,' he writes in *Style and the Man*.

(**Onassis**) The Greek shipping magnate Aristotle Onassis wore what appears to be an unusual variation of the four-in-hand in which the knot itself is completely hidden from view. The result may be effected by bringing the active end of the finished four-in-hand behind to the right and out through the centre $L \otimes R \odot L \otimes C \odot TR \otimes C \odot$, allowing it to drape over the front. The result is satisfactory only when used with a collar sufficiently spread to accommodate the full width of the tie. The Onassis 'still has a certain popularity along Seventh Avenue' in New York, reported the *New York Times* in 1989.

*Aristotle Onassis wearing his trademark variation
on the four-in-hand.*

Five-Move Knots

Knot 3 (Kelvin)

L⊙R⊗L⊙R⊗C⊙T

The Kelvin is an extension of the Oriental (1), in which the active end is wrapped a second time around the passive end before being brought through the centre. The result is a narrow, elegant knot which is slightly fuller and more symmetrical than the four-in-hand (2). If any knot will pose a threat to the prevalence of the four-in-hand, the Kelvin is the most likely candidate.

(Diagonal) When the Kelvin is tied so that the active end is passed through both of its previous winds (L⊙R⊗L⊙R⊗C⊙TT), the conformation collapses into an unusual knot which, when worn back-to-front, is known as the Diagonal. The face of the knot is formed by two segments of the tie which overlap diagonally. The same knot, achieved by an alternative sequence of moves, can be found in *The Book of Ties* (1985) by Davide Mosconi and Riccardo Villarosa.

The TT ending.

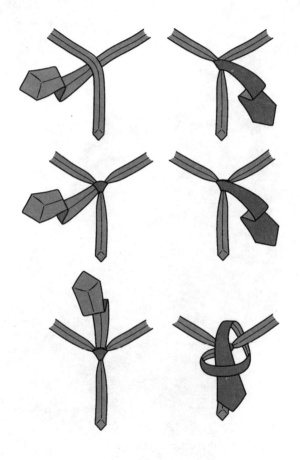

Fred Astaire's four-in-hand tie and collar pin are as meticulous as his footwork.

Narrow knots – like knots 1, 2, 3 and 6 – can be successfully accompanied by a collar bar or collar pin, a practice which was common during the first half of the twentieth century and enjoys a small following today. The bar bridges the points of the collar underneath the knot, forcing the knot up and outwards and causing the tie to billow away from the shirt.

The early popularity of bars and pins largely originated from the need to secure the ill-knotted four-in-hands of the time. The 'Major' spends considerable effort outlining the correct way to insert a tie pin in *Clothes and the Man* (1900), and relates the dire consequences of failing to do so: 'the lady beside him fainted, he spoilt a good collar, tie, and shirt, and the engagement is now off,' he warns. 'That will show you the folly of wearing your scarf-pin in the wrong place. The right place to put it is about two inches away from the knot.'

Five-Move Knots

Two Centres

Knot 4 (Nicky)

L⊙C⊗R⊙L⊗C⊙T

The earliest published evidence of the Nicky can be found in Mosconi and Villarosa's *The Book of Ties*. Ernesto Curami, of the Italian tie shop Nicky, advocated it in Milan. 'At one time I even had brochures printed to explain to my customers how to tie it.' It seems, however, that the knot did not gain popularity outside Italy.

Some years later, in 1989, David Kelsall mis-tied the Pratt knot (5) illustrated in the *Daily Telegraph*. By his fortuitous mistake he unknowingly rediscovered the Nicky, which he later submitted to the *Sunday Telegraph* in 1991. The knot was referred to as a 'super-Pratt', a suggestion rejected by Dr. Kelsall, who named the knot the Olney (pronounced Oney) after the town in Buckinghamshire in which he lives. The knot's primary advantage over the Pratt is that it unties cleanly, leaving no residual overhand knot when the passive end is removed, a result of transposing the final L⊙R⊗ pair.

Soon afterwards, the Guild of British Tie Makers offered a case of claret to anyone who could devise a knot that is both 'elegant and practical'. The Pratt and the Olney were (wrongly) discounted by the Guild as 'slight variation[s] on the popular half-Windsor'. They are not. The claret remains to be awarded.

The Nicky is an elegant and versatile knot, intermediate in size between the four-in-hand (2) and the half-Windsor (7). Like the Oriental (1), the knot begins with the tie inside-out around the neck.

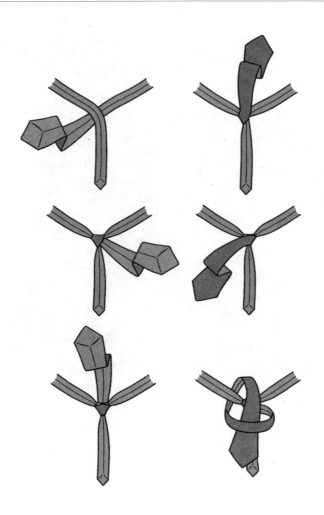

Classic James Bond: white shirt and black knit silk tie.

Knot 5 (Pratt) L⊙C⊗L⊙R⊗C⊙T

Apart from the long-established four-in-hand (2), Windsor (31) and half-Windsor (7), the Pratt (sometimes known as the Shelby) is the only knot which has received widespread attention. It was revealed in the *New York Times* and the *Daily Telegraph* in 1989. Jerry Pratt, its American inventor, used the knot for 30 years before Don Shelby publicised it on local television. The Pratt knot is a non-releasing derivative of the Nicky (4) and is similar in size and shape.

Before the Pratt became prominent, it was occasionally worn in America from as early as the Second World War, usually under the name of reverse half-Windsor. This name is misleading (not to mention long-winded); the Pratt is no more the reverse of the half-Windsor than the half-Windsor is half of the Windsor.

(**Vismara**) Mosconi and Villarosa describe an unusual knot detailed in a 1950s publication by the Milanese company Vismara. The instructions presented in the end pages of *The Book of Ties*, however, amount to the Pratt knot worn back to front.

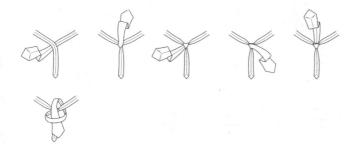

Six-Move Knots

Knot 6 (Victoria)

L⊗R⊙L⊗R⊙L⊗C⊙T

The Victoria relates to the four-in-hand (2) in the same way as the Kelvin (3) relates to the Oriental (1): the active end makes a second revolution before finishing to the centre and through the outer turn just made. The result is a knot similar in shape to the four-in-hand but with added bulk, which can prove useful for thin or well-worn ties.

The Victoria is usually described according to a variation known as the Prince Albert (below). It was published in its own right, however, in *The Ashley Book of Knots* (1944) by Clifford Ashley. 'If the material of a Four-in-Hand tie lacks substance it may be passed three times instead of twice when starting the knot. The

Joseph Conrad in a Prince Albert.

end, however, in the final tucking down is passed only under the last or upper turn.' Of the over 3,000 knots catalogued in the treatise, only two others are tie knots: the Oriental and the four-in-hand.

(**Prince Albert**) When the active end is passed through both the first and second turnings ($L \otimes R \odot L \otimes R \odot L \otimes C \odot TT$), the Victoria is known as the Prince Albert. There is, however, no evidence that the consort to Queen Victoria actually wore this knot; it seems unlikely, since he died in 1861 and the four-in-hand tie was not fashionable until the 1860s.

The Prince Albert, though similar to the Victoria in shape, can be identified by the partly visible first turning over the passive end. Indeed, it is not properly executed otherwise. The knot has a small but definite following, if only because of its originality. 'The Prince Albert is the prime example of a highly original knot which never seems ridiculous – quite the contrary. To tell the truth, it is my favourite knot for four-in-hand ties,' writes Chaille.

The standard four-in-hand knot (tie: Austin Reed)

Knot 1 (*Oriental*)

Left and opposite: All close-up photographs of tie knots show ties supplied by T.M. Lewin and all ties are of exactly the same weight and weave. Above: Tie: Gieves & Hawkes.

Knot 2 (*Four-in-hand*)

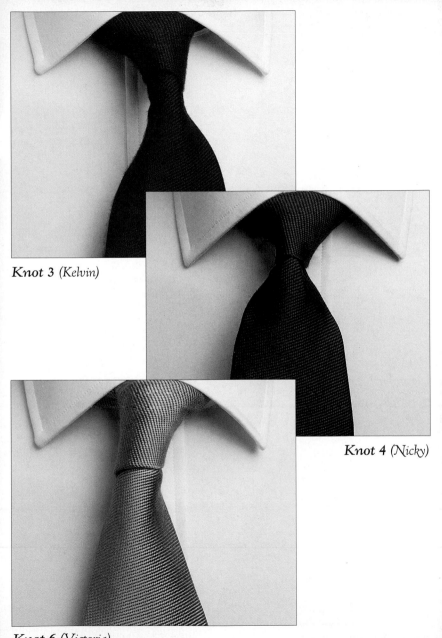

Knot 3 (*Kelvin*)

Knot 4 (*Nicky*)

Knot 6 (*Victoria*)

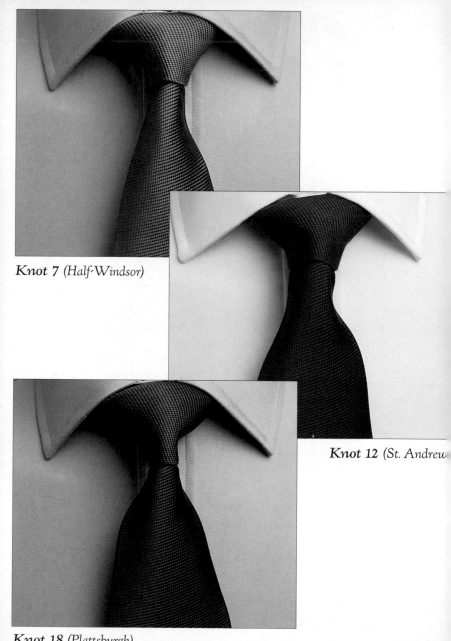

Knot 7 (Half-Windsor)

Knot 12 (St. Andrew

Knot 18 (Plattsburgh)

Knot 23 *(Cavendish)*

The manikin debates the merits of (left to right) the four-in-hand, Plattsburgh and Kelvin (ties all from Gieves & Hawkes).

Knot 31 *(Windsor)*

Knot 44 (*Grantchester*)

Above: All ties from Gieves & Hawkes. Right: The manikin wears the largest and smallest of the aesthetic knots in a tie supplied by Tie Rack. Next page: All the aesthetic knots in ties from T. M. Lewin.

Knot 54 (*Hanover*)

Knot 78 (Balthus)

From Oriental ...

... to Balthus

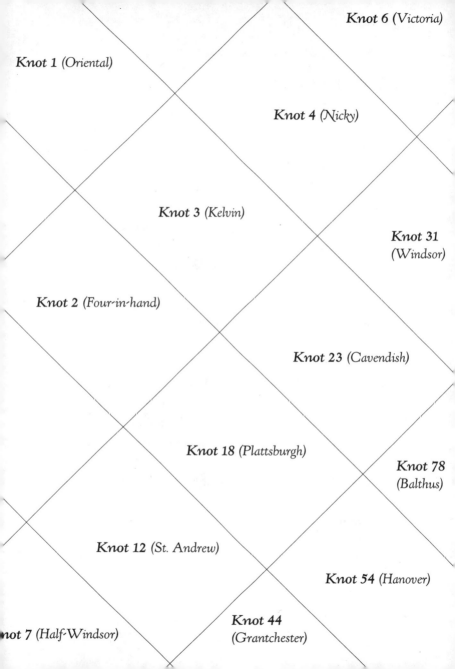

Six-Move Knots   Two Centres
Knot 7 (Half-Windsor)   L⊗R⊙C⊗L⊙R⊗C⊙T

The half-Windsor is arguably the most versatile of all tie knots. Its intermediate size between the four-in-hand (2) and the Windsor (31) suits most collars, and its moderate, symmetrical shape satisfies most tastes. The knot can be discreet in a lightweight or well-worn tie, or substantial in heavy woven silk or wool.

Despite what its name suggests, the half-Windsor is not half the size of the Windsor but rather three-quarters. (The alternative would imply that the Windsor designates the rather substantial knot *L⊗R⊙C⊗L⊙R⊗C⊙L⊗R⊙C⊗L⊙R⊗C⊙T*). This casts suspicion on the other half of its etymology. There is no evidence that the half-Windsor derived from the Windsor, though the authors have yet to learn of the half-Windsor's use before the Windsor's.

'When the fabric of the tie permits (if it is silk twill or a supple Jacquard silk, for example), a beautiful effect can be obtained by using the index finger to press a slight convex cavity into the tie just below the knot. The French call this little hollow a *cuillère*, which means spoon or scoop,' explains Chaille. In English the hollow is called a dimple or a fluke, and it can be important – some would say crucial – to a well-tied knot. In fact it is best suited to wide ties or ties which do not taper sufficiently to be narrow near the opening of the knot, as they allow deeper and more stable dimples. An example can be seen in Roosevelt's tie on page 84; dimples have intentionally been left out of the principal aesthetic knots in the colour plates to aid clarity.

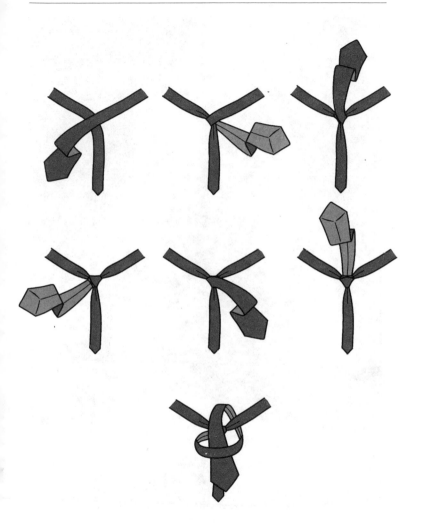

President Franklin Roosevelt.

Knot 8 L⊗R⊙C⊗R⊙L⊗C⊙T

Many tie knots do not have a definitive definition, largely because their origins are unknown. The *Oxford English Dictionary*, for instance, tells us only that a four-in-hand is 'tied in a loose knot with hanging ends'. Unfortunately, more relevant publications tend to contradict each other. Tie knots are, invariably, learnt through tradition.

Not surprisingly, different men know different knots under the same name. Such knots usually differ by the transposition of one or more *RL* (or *LR*) groups, in which case the knots are called derivatives of each other. Knot 8 is a derivative of the half-Windsor (7) and is sometimes tied in lieu of it.

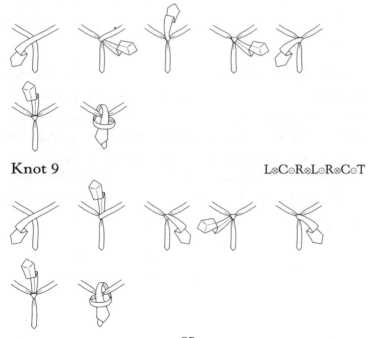

Knot 9 L⊗C⊙R⊗L⊙R⊗C⊙T

Knot 10   L⊗C∘L⊗R∘L⊗C∘T

It seems that a number of publications have unwittingly identified this knot as the half-Windsor (7), most likely by blind repetition of an initial blunder. The knot is last in its class, not least owing to its asymmetry. As George V admonished his son Edward, Prince of Wales, 'I wonder whose idea that was, as anything more unsmart I never saw.'

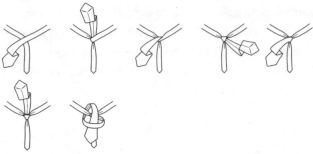

Seven-Move Knots   One Centre

Knot 11   L∘R⊗L∘R⊗L∘R⊗C∘T

For the first time we encounter a class of knots none of which is aesthetic. The active end in the Victoria (6) makes two and a half revolutions around the passive end; wrapped thrice around, knot 11 is sufficiently cylindrical to be of questionable taste. More practically, it is unbalanced and inclined to lose its shape. Classes (8,1) and (9,1) present the same problem to a greater extreme.

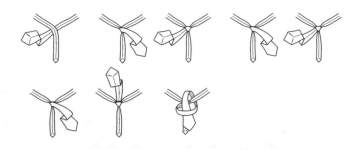

He does give a damn: an elegant Clark Gable.

Seven-Move Knots　　　　　　· Two Centres
Knot 12 (St. Andrew)　　　L⊙R⊗L⊙C⊗R⊙L⊗C⊙T

The St. Andrew lies between the half-Windsor (7) and the Windsor (31) in size but is more narrowly shaped than either. It sits slightly askew in the collar, although it is not as asymmetrical as the four-in-hand. When tautly tied, it has considerable depth which allows it to stand up and drape well. 'It's got a charming dimple and is pleasantly flamboyant – not for an accountant but good for a merchant banker,' observes Mark Henderson, managing director of the Savile Row tailors Gieves and Hawkes.

A properly executed knot causes the tie to protrude slightly from the neck, forming a hollow before it returns to the chest. This effect may be achieved by gently tightening the tie around the neck and pulling the knot up into the collar. The extent to which a knot will cooperate depends on its backing, the bulk of material in the back of the knot.

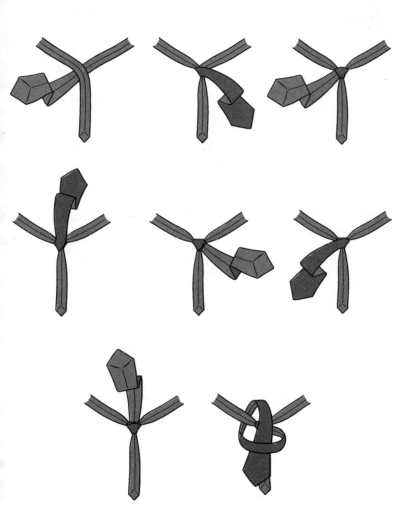

Knot 13

L∘R⊗C∘L⊗R∘L⊗C∘T

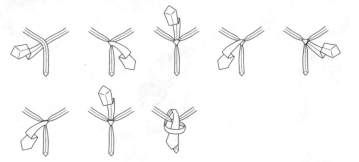

Knot 14

L∘R⊗L∘C⊗L∘R⊗C∘T

This is a non-releasing derivative of the St. Andrew (12).

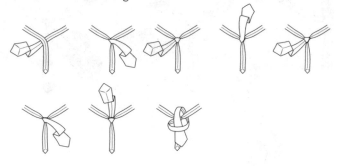

Knot 15

L∘R⊗C∘R⊗L∘R⊗C∘T

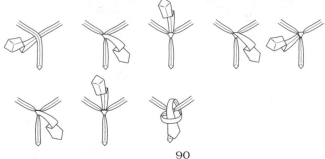

Knot 16

When terminated with *TT* rather than *T*, knots 16 and 17 are smaller versions of the Christensen (**25**, **27**), whose hallmark is its cruciform motif. As with the Christensen, the cross effect is best achieved with straight or narrow ties.

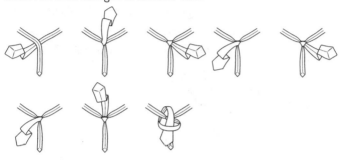

Knot 17 See knot 16.

L⊙C⊗L⊙R⊗L⊙R⊗C⊙T

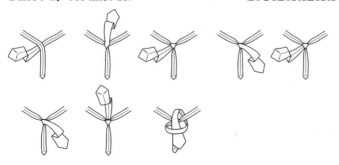

91

Seven-Move Knots   Three Centres
Knot 18 (Plattsburgh)   L⊙C⊗R⊙C⊗L⊙R⊗C⊙T

In contrast to its narrow next-of-kin the St. Andrew (12), the Plattsburgh produces a symmetric knot characterised by a broad, inverted cone with a narrow opening. It is the only modestly sized knot to exhibit the breadth of larger, if more conspicuous, tie knots.

The authors favour the Plattsburgh, usually in light- or medium-weight ties with a semi-cutaway collar. The knot is perhaps most effective in bringing back to life well-worn ties otherwise left to hang in the closet.

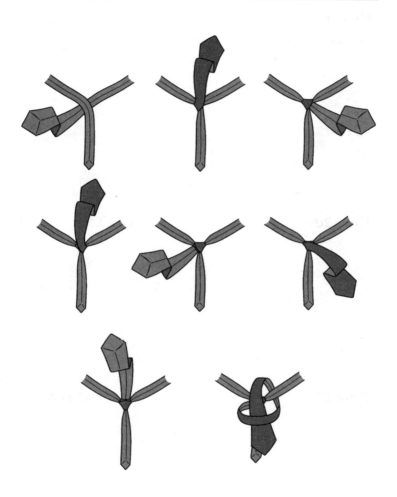

Knot 19

L⊙C⊗R⊙C⊗R⊙L⊗C⊙T

This is a self-releasing derivative of the Plattsburgh (18).

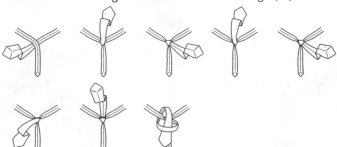

Knot 20

L⊙C⊗L⊙C⊗R⊙L⊗C⊙T

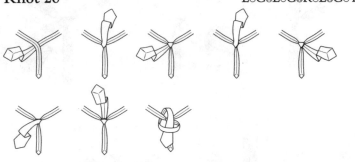

Knot 21

L⊙C⊗L⊙C⊗L⊙R⊗C⊙T

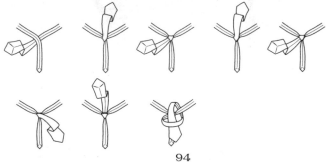

Eight-Move Knots
Knot 22

One Centre
L⊗R⊙L⊗R⊙L⊗R⊙L⊗C⊙T

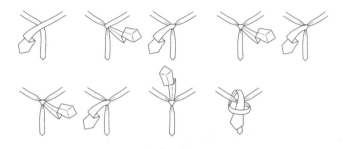

Cary Grant: nice dimples.

Eight-Move Knots   Two Centres
Knot 23 (Cavendish)   L⊗R⊙L⊗C⊙R⊗L⊙R⊗C⊙T

While the Cavendish is the same size as the Windsor (31), it has an altogether different appearance. An inspection of its sequence reveals that the knot may be considered a concatenation of two four-in-hands (2), one a mirror image of the other. This gives it a similar shape: like the four-in-hand, it forms a narrow triangle. The slight asymmetry follows from the second four-in-hand which, tied further down the active end, is dominant. 'A four-in-hand with substance,' Luke Howard, who has tried most of the 85 knots presented here, describes the Cavendish. 'I'll be damned if I tie a four-in-hand again.' This knot is a prime example of a large knot suitable for narrow collars, though it fills a spread collar equally well.

The appearance of a knot depends as much on the texture and weight of the tie as on the sequence used to tie it. Tied in a lightweight tie, the Cavendish could pass for a four-in-hand in a more substantial cloth. The Duke of Windsor used specially tailored thick ties knotted with a four-in-hand to produce what appeared to be a Windsor knot. As a rule, heavy woven, knitted and wool ties act to exaggerate a knot's size; twill and satin ties produce smaller knots. With age, however, the segment of the tie where the knot is made will grow supple and pliant, producing tighter and smaller knots. In all cases, the choice of knot must be informed by the material with which it is to be constructed.

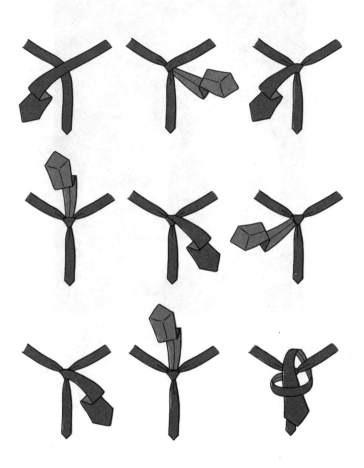

Marlene Dietrich: she couldn't help it.

Knot 24   L⊗R⊙L⊗R⊙C⊗L⊙R⊗C⊙T

Knot 25 (Christensen) $L\otimes R\odot C\otimes L\odot R\otimes L\odot R\otimes C\odot T$

In 1917 the Swedish mail order company Stralin and Persson displayed a beautiful knot characterised by an unusual cruciform structure. Unfortunately, the catalogue in which it appeared did not provide instructions. Some time later, it was republished on behalf of the Swedish tie maker Amanda Christensen, and is now known as the Christensen, or cross knot.

Though we cannot be sure, it is probable that the Christensen is equivalent to knots 25 or 27, with the active end passed through both of the final turns rather than one (i.e., $L\otimes R\odot C\otimes L\odot R\otimes L\odot R\otimes C\odot TT$). Other knots also display the narrow cruciform motif when finished in the same way: two of size 7 (knots 16 and 17) and two of size 9 (knots 45 and 49). These, however, begin with the tie inside-out, a technique which was uncommon until the later part of the twentieth century.

The Christensen was originally intended for straight ties, as the illustration shows; this ensures that the crossing of the blades is visible. It is rare to find straight ties today, but a narrow one should be equally effective.

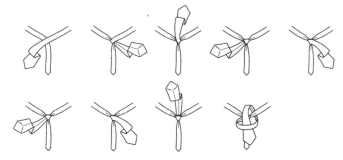

Knot 26

L⊗R⊙L⊗R⊙C⊗R⊙L⊗C⊙T

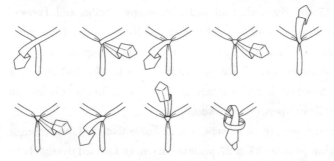

Knot 27 (Christensen) See knot 25.

L⊗R⊙C⊗R⊙L⊗R⊙L⊗C⊙T

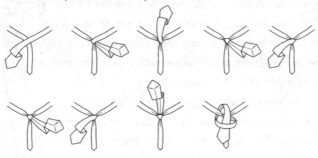

Knot 28

L⊗C⊙R⊗L⊙R⊗L⊙R⊗C⊙T

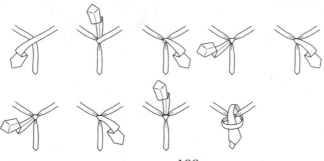

Knot 29

L⊗R⊙L⊗C⊙L⊗R⊙L⊗C⊙T

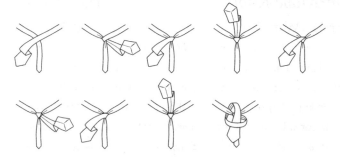

Knot 30

L⊗C⊙L⊗R⊙L⊗R⊙L⊗C⊙T

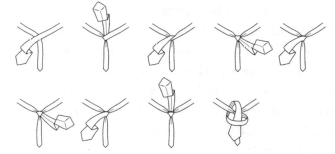

Eight-Move Knots

Knot 31 (Windsor)

Three Centres

L⊗C⊙R⊗L⊙C⊗R⊙L⊗C⊙T

When the trend-setting Prince of Wales, later the Duke of Windsor, took a liking to large tie knots in the 1930s, it did not go unnoticed. Within years men everywhere wore ties 'fastened with the popular Windsor knot, larger than the usual four-in-hand, to fill the space of the wide spread collar,' wrote *Esquire* in 1940. Discarding the ubiquitous four-in-hand (2) in favour of the larger knot was, at the time, a conspicuous gesture. But it was an elegant one, and the knot has never really fallen out of fashion since.

It is widely accepted that the Duke of Windsor did not invent the knot which bears his name. Indeed, he did not even wear it. His trademark large knot was effected not by a complicated sequence but rather by the specially made thick ties with which he tied them. In his memoirs *A Family Album* (1960), the Duke explains that 'the so-called "Windsor knot" in the tie was adopted in America at a later date. It was I believe regulation wear for G.I.s during the war, when American college boys adopted it too. But in fact I was in no way responsible for this. The knot to which Americans gave my name was a double knot in a narrow tie – a "slim Jim" as it is sometimes called. It is true that I myself have always preferred a large knot, as looking better than a small one, so during the nineteen twenties I devised, in conclave with Mr. Sandford, a tie always of the broad variety which was reinforced by an extra thickness of material to produce this effect. As far as I know this particular fashion has never been followed in America or elsewhere.'

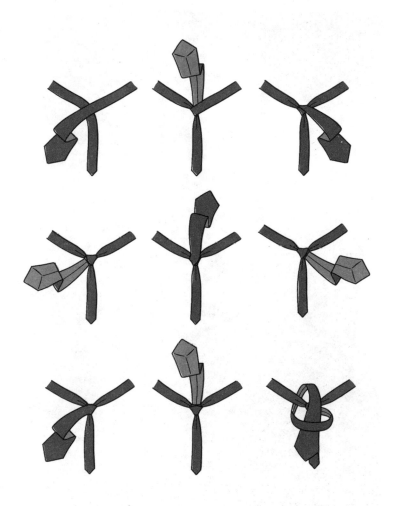

Frank Sinatra: his way was a Windsor.

Enthusiasm for the large knot invented by the public continued to grow throughout the 1940s. The name 'Windsor' persisted, even when the Queen's cousin Lord Lichfield photographed the Duke tying his tie in the 1960s in an effort to dispel the long-standing myth. The knot remains popular today, especially among southern Europeans, who display a variety of tie knots sadly absent in Britain.

The Windsor produces a solid, triangular knot which, needless to say, sits best in a Windsor (spread) collar – something the Duke did in fact wear. For those who prefer a less substantial look, the Windsor can always produce a more modestly sized knot in a lightweight tie or a tie made supple by years of use.

Knot 32   L⊗C⊙L⊗R⊙C⊗L⊙R⊗C⊙T

Like 'half-Windsor' and other knot names, 'Windsor' has been used to describe more than one knot. Invariably, these are limited to derivatives of the Windsor effected by the transposition of one or more *RL* (or *LR*) groups. Knots 32 (especially), 33 and 35 are also known as the Windsor. Their subtleties of difference have no doubt resulted in a preference for each.

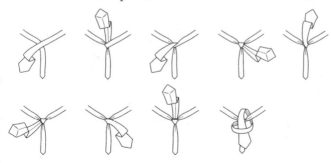

Knot 33 See knot 32.

L⊗C⊙R⊗L⊙C⊗L⊙R⊗C⊙T

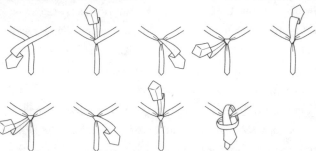

Knot 34

L⊗R⊙C⊗L⊙C⊗R⊙L⊗C⊙T

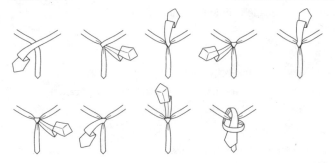

Knot 35 See knot 32.

L⊗C⊙L⊗R⊙C⊗R⊙L⊗C⊙T

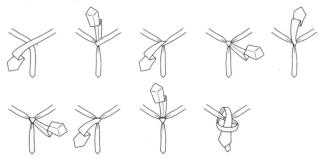

Knot 36

$L \otimes R \odot C \otimes R \odot C \otimes L \odot R \otimes C \odot T$

  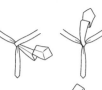 

Knot 37

$L \otimes R \odot C \otimes L \odot C \otimes L \odot R \otimes C \odot T$

Knot 38

$L \otimes C \odot R \otimes C \odot L \otimes R \odot L \otimes C \odot T$

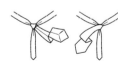

Knot 39

L⊗R⊙C⊗R⊙C⊗R⊙L⊗C⊙T

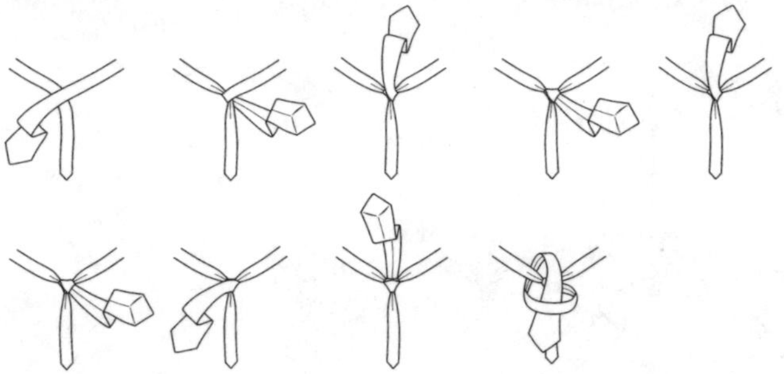

Knot 40

L⊗C⊙L⊗C⊙R⊗L⊙R⊗C⊙T

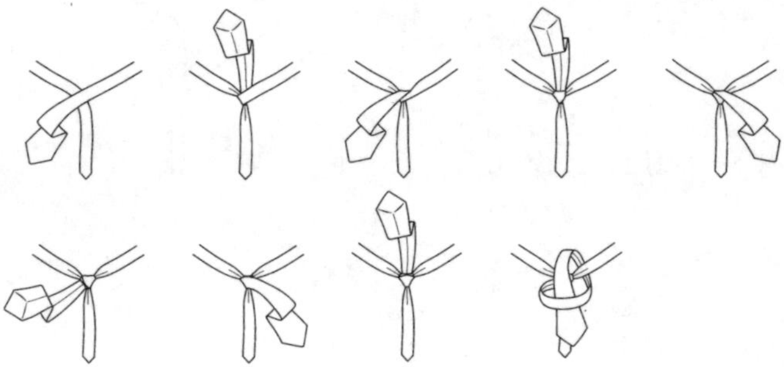

Knot 41

L⊗C⊙R⊗C⊙R⊗L⊙R⊗C⊙T

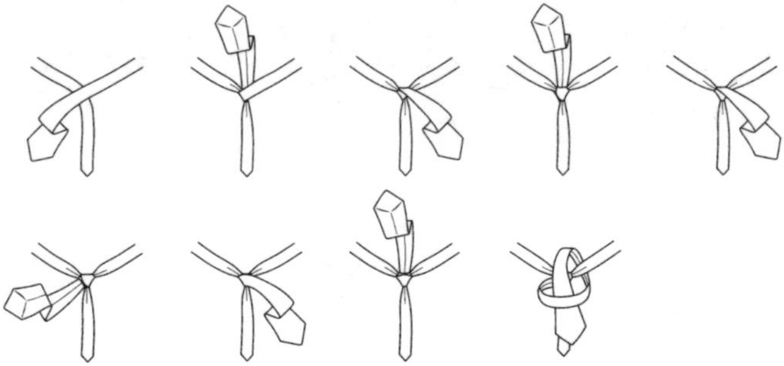

Knot 42

L⊗C⊙L⊗C⊙L⊗R⊙L⊗C⊙T

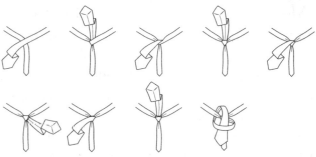

Nine-Move Knots

Knot 43

One Centre

L⊙R⊗L⊙R⊗L⊙R⊗L⊙R⊗C⊙T

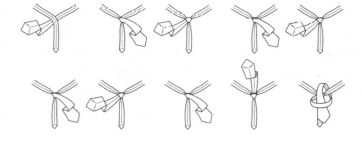

Nine-Move Knots   Two Centres

Knot 44 (Grantchester)   L⊙R⊗L⊙R⊗C⊙L⊗R⊙L⊗C⊙T

Large knots have had a following ever since the Duke of Windsor exaggerated his four-in-hand with purpose-tailored thick ties. 'The big-knot tie came into prominence during the thirties,' wrote *Esquire's Encyclopedia of 20th Century Men's Fashion*, and the large knot remained fashionable 'well into the fifties and sixties, when it slipped into oblivion with the advent of the wide tie'. With the return of men's clothes and ties to their natural proportions, the desire for a substantial knot – Windsor or otherwise – came with it.

Among the three principal nine-move knots (44, 54, 78), the Grantchester is the narrowest and least conspicuous. It may be considered a concatenation of the Kelvin (3) and a mirror image of the four-in-hand (2), which gives an indication of its shape if not its size.

Larger knots require a greater length of tie, and care must be made to start them sufficiently near the passive end so that the completed tie is the appropriate length. This places a practical limit on knot size: while it differs from tie to tie, knots of nine moves or less should not present material shortages. (Rather luckily for us; were the cutoff 10 moves, our 85 knots would leap to 170.)

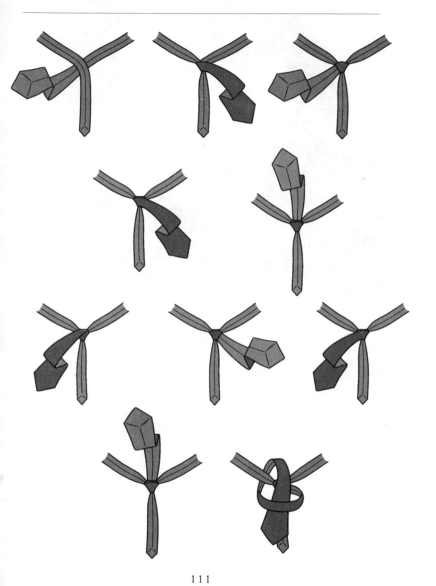

Laurel and Hardy: no fine messes in their matching tie knots.

Knot 45 $\quad\quad\quad\quad\quad$ L⊙R⊗L⊙C⊗R⊙L⊗R⊙L⊗C⊙T

When terminated with TT instead of T, knots 45 and 49 exhibit the same cross motif as the Christensen (25, 27), but with added bulk. They are best executed with straight or narrow ties.

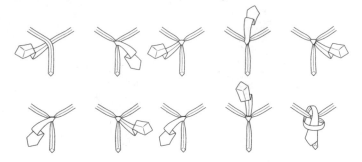

Knot 46

$L \circ R \otimes L \circ R \otimes L \circ C \otimes R \circ L \otimes C \circ T$

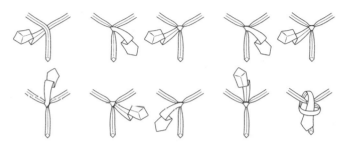

Knot 47

$L \circ R \otimes C \circ L \otimes R \circ L \otimes R \circ L \otimes C \circ T$

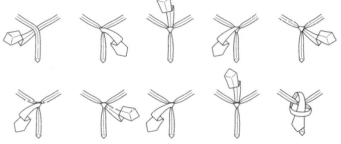

Knot 48

$L \circ R \otimes L \circ R \otimes C \circ R \otimes L \circ R \otimes C \circ T$

This is a (non-releasing) derivative of the Grantchester (44).

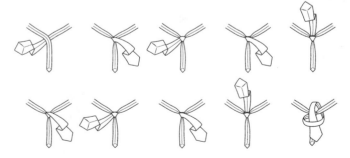

Knot 49 See knot 45.

L∘R⊗L∘C⊗L∘R⊗L∘R⊗C∘T

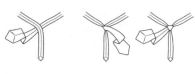

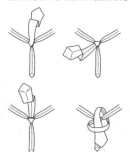

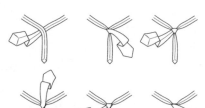

Knot 50

L∘R⊗L∘R⊗L∘C⊗L∘R⊗C∘T

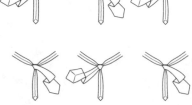

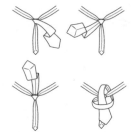

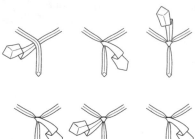

Knot 51

L∘R⊗C∘R⊗L∘R⊗L∘R⊗C∘T

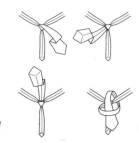

Knot 52

L⊙C⊗R⊙L⊗R⊙L⊗R⊙L⊗C⊙T

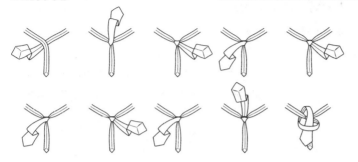

Knot 53

L⊙C⊗L⊙R⊗L⊙R⊗L⊙R⊗C⊙T

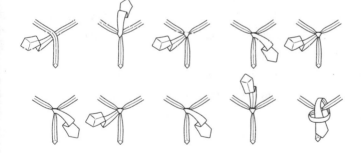

Nine-Move Knots

Three Centres

Knot 54 (Hanover)

L⊙R⊗C⊙L⊗R⊙C⊗L⊙R⊗C⊙T

A comparison of their sequences will show that the Hanover is the natural extension of the Oriental (1) and the half-Windsor (7). The construction of all three is straightforward and elegant: the active end is woven over and under the three spokes of the tie in a counter-clockwise direction, making one, two and three revolutions, respectively. As a result, these are the only knots with perfect symmetry and balance. Like the half-Windsor, the Hanover is a symmetrical, triangular knot, though in size it exceeds the Windsor (31).

It is advisable that any broad knot be worn only with what the English call cutaway or semi-cutaway collars, as any other style would crop the corners. Such an unfortunate oversight would have the double effect of concealing the shape of the knot and forcing the collar to flare away from the shirt to accommodate it (men in button-down collars, be warned). Similarly, narrow knots are well suited to narrow and button-down collars. On cutaway collars they can appear insubstantial, though this has done little to discourage the common combination of the two. However the tie is tied, the knot and collar should be in proportion.

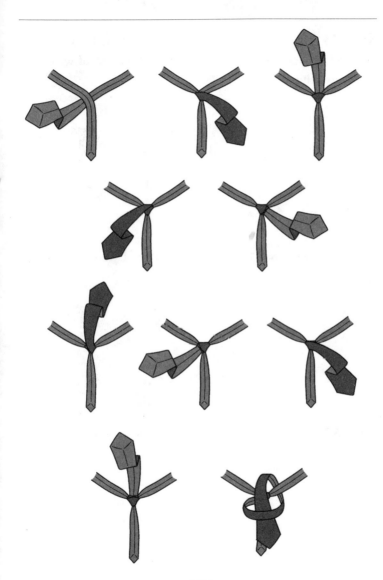

Knot 55

L⊙R⊗C⊙R⊗L⊙C⊗R⊙L⊗C⊙T

Knots 55, 56 and 59 are derivatives of the Hanover, of which 55 and 56 are self-releasing.

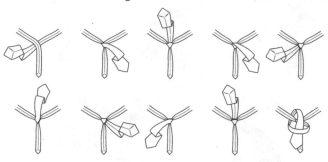

Knot 56 See knot 55.

L⊙R⊗C⊙L⊗R⊙C⊗R⊙L⊗C⊙T

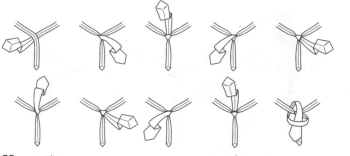

Knot 57

L⊙C⊗R⊙L⊗R⊙C⊗L⊙R⊗C⊙T

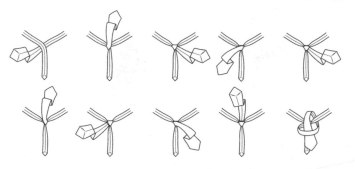

The Duke of Windsor not wearing a Windsor knot.

Knot 58

L∘C⊗R∘L⊗C∘R∘L∘R⊗C∘T

Knot 59 See knot 55.

L∘R⊗C∘R⊗L∘C⊗L∘R⊗C∘T

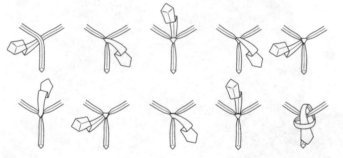

Knot 60

L∘C⊗R∘L⊗R∘C⊗R∘L⊗C∘T

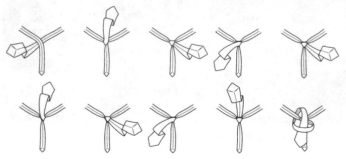

Knot 61

L∘R⊗L∘C⊗R∘C⊗L∘R⊗C∘T

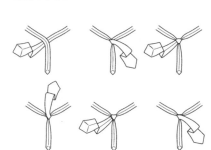

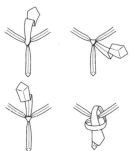

Knot 62

L∘R⊗C∘L⊗C∘R⊗L∘R⊗C∘T

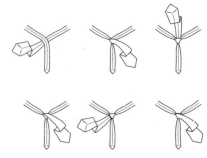

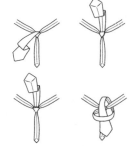

Knot 63

L∘R⊗L∘C⊗R∘C⊗R∘L⊗C∘T

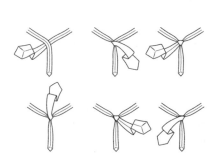

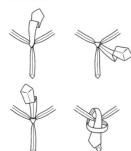

Knot 64

L∘R⊗C∘R⊗C∘L∘R∘L⊗C∘T

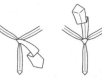

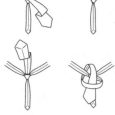
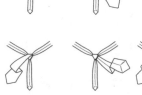

Knot 65

L∘C⊗L∘R⊗C∘R⊗L∘R⊗C∘T

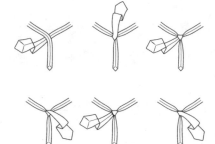
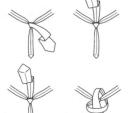

Knot 66

L∘C⊗R∘C⊗L∘R⊗L∘R⊗C∘T

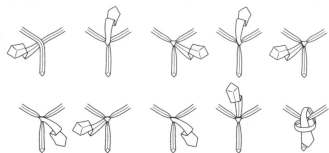

Knot 67

L∘C⊗R∘C⊗R∘L⊗R∘L⊗C∘T

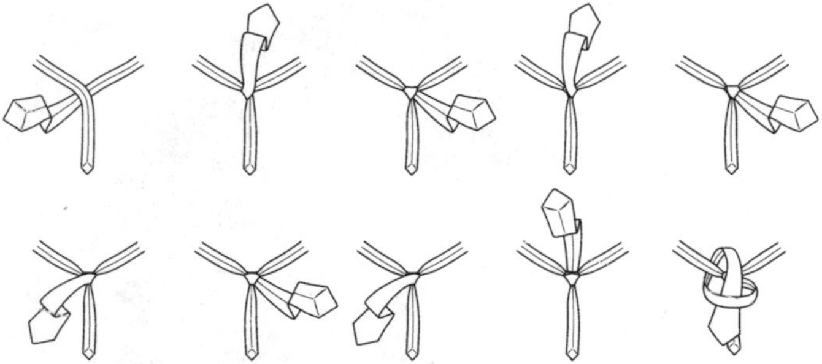

Knot 68

L∘C⊗L∘R⊗L∘C⊗R∘L⊗C∘T

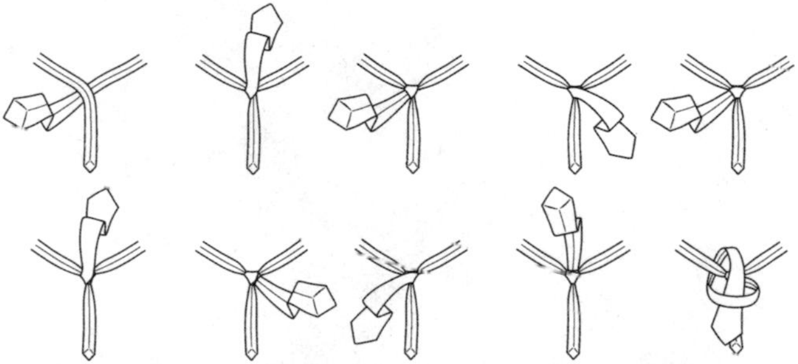

Knot 69

L∘C⊗L∘R⊗C∘L⊗R∘L⊗C∘T

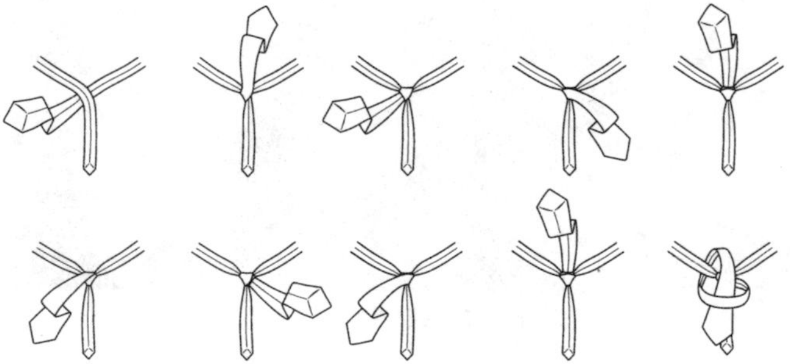

Rupert Brooke, 1913.

Knot 70

L⊙C⊗R⊙L⊗C⊙L⊗R⊙L⊗C⊙T

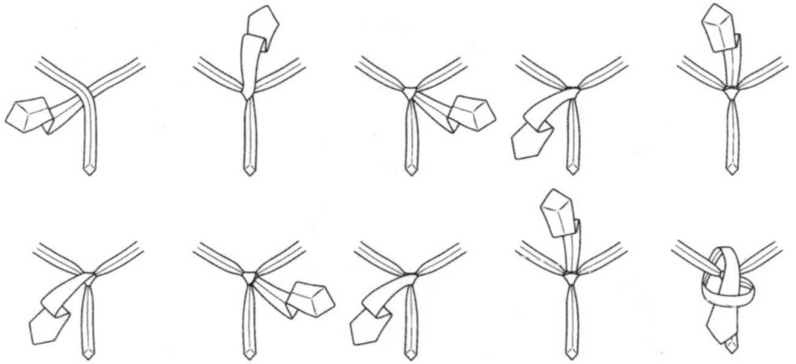

Knot 71

L⊙C⊗L⊙R⊗L⊙C⊗L⊙R⊗C⊙T

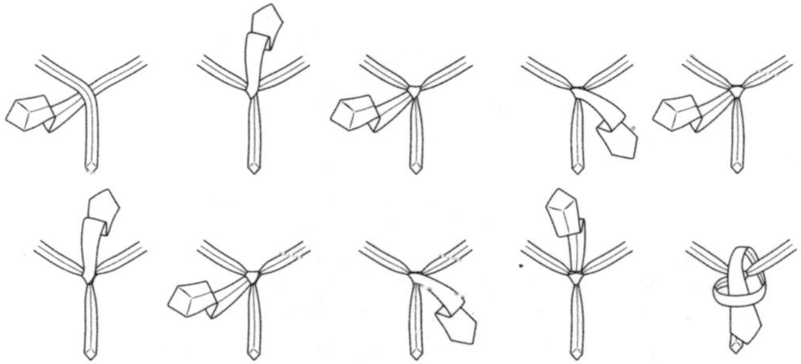

Knot 72

L⊙R⊗L⊙C⊗L⊙C⊗R⊙L⊗C⊙T

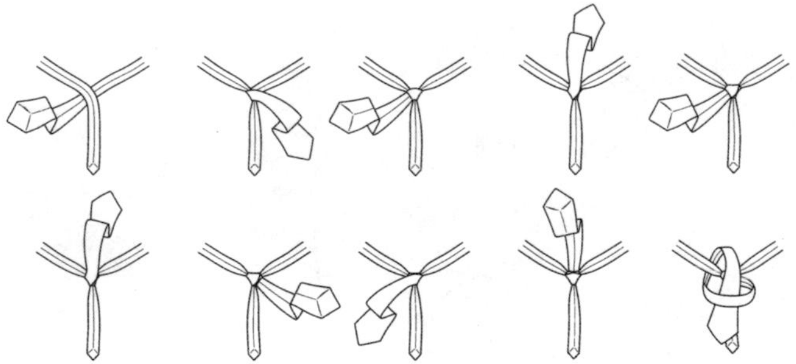

Knot 73

L⊙R⊗C⊙L⊗C⊙L⊗R⊙L⊗C⊙T

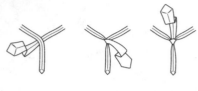 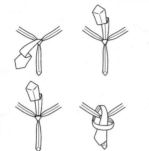

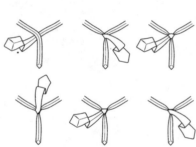 

Knot 74

L⊙R⊗L⊙C⊗L⊙C⊗L⊙R⊗C⊙T

 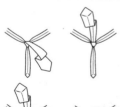

Knot 75

L⊙R⊗C⊙R⊗C⊙R⊗L⊙R⊗C⊙T

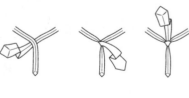

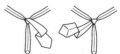

Knot 76

L⊙C⊗L⊙C⊗R⊙L⊗R⊙L⊗C⊙T

 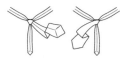 

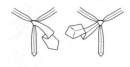 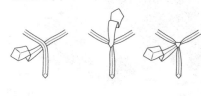 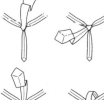

Knot 77

L⊙C⊗L⊙C⊗L⊙R⊗L⊙R⊗C⊙T

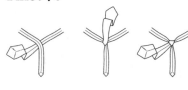

Nine-Move Knots

Knot 78 (Balthus)

The Balthus belongs to the last and broadest of the knot classes. It is a direct extension of the Plattsburgh (18) and possesses a similarly broad, conical shape.

The manner of a knot's execution can be as important to its appearance as the choice of knot itself. Whichever knot is used, a tie should not be so tightly tied that the knot is deformed, nor so loosely arranged that it is nondescript. The former (and lesser) evil creates a small knot from a not-so-small sequence. The latter is usually the result of negligence and is aggravated to malice when applied to a big sequence.

The artist Balthus exhibiting his unconventional creation, 1933.

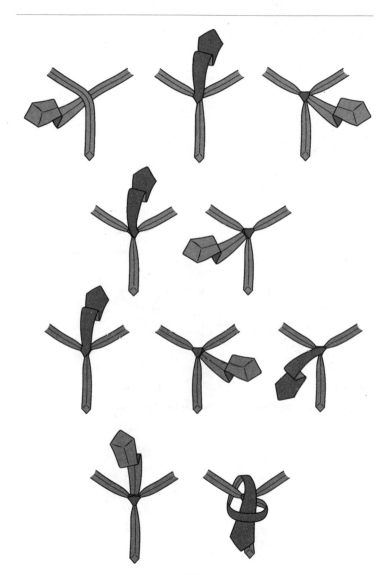

Knot 79

L⊙C⊗L⊙C⊗R⊙C⊗L⊙R⊗C⊙T

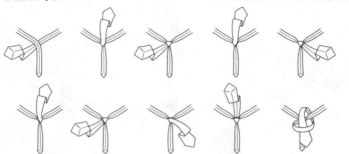

Knot 80

L⊙C⊗R⊙C⊗R⊙C⊗L⊙R⊗C⊙T

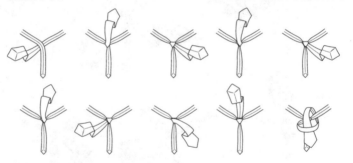

Knot 81

L⊙C⊗R⊙C⊗L⊙C⊗L⊙R⊗C⊙T

This is a non-releasing derivative of the Balthus.

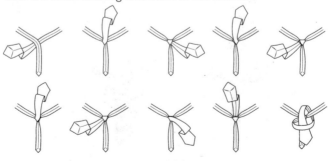

Knot 82

L⊙C⊗L⊙C⊗R⊙C⊗R⊙L⊗C⊙T

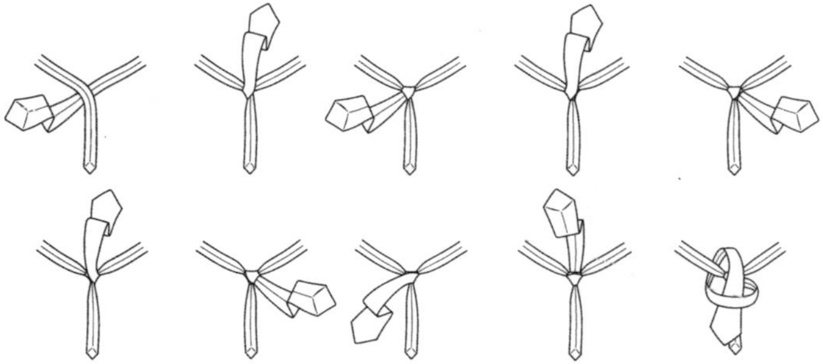

Knot 83

L⊙C⊗R⊙C⊗R⊙C⊗R⊙L⊗C⊙T

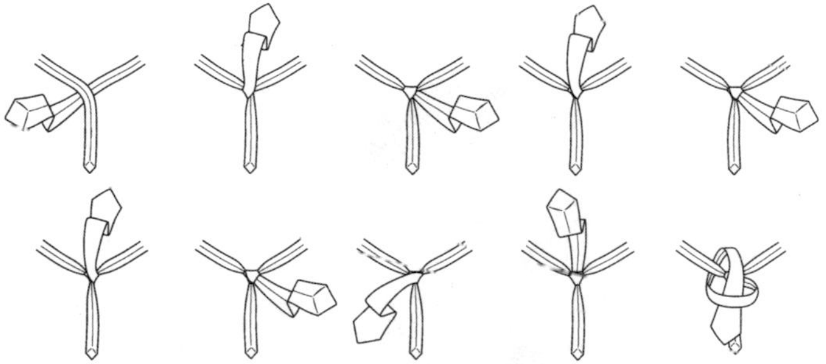

Knot 84

L⊙C⊗L⊙C⊗L⊙C⊗R⊙L⊗C⊙T

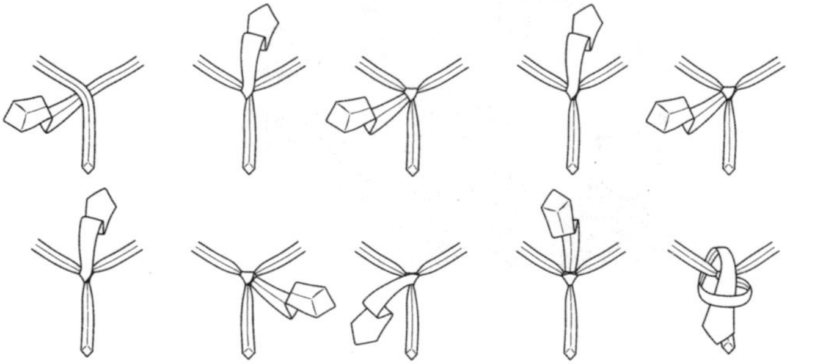

Knot 85

L∘C⊗L∘C⊗L∘C⊗L∘R⊗C∘T

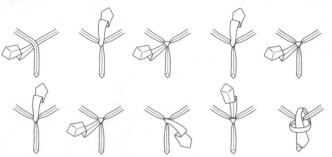

Summary of 85 Tie Knots

Summary of tie knots, characterised, from left, by knot number n, size h, centre γ, sequence, symmetry s, balance b, knotted status k and name, if any.

n	h	γ	sequence	s	b	k	name
1	3	1	L∘R⊗C∘T	0	0	y	Oriental
2	4	1	L⊗R∘L⊗C∘T	1	1	n	four-in-hand
3	5	1	L∘R⊗L∘R⊗C∘T	0	2	y	Kelvin
4	5	2	L∘C⊗R∘L⊗C∘T	1	0	n	Nicky
5	5	2	L∘C⊗L∘R⊗C∘T	1	1	y	Pratt
6	6	1	L⊗R∘L⊗R∘L⊗C∘T	1	3	n	Victoria
7	6	2	L⊗R∘C⊗L∘R⊗C∘T	0	0	y	half-Windsor
8	6	2	L⊗R∘C⊗R∘L⊗C∘T	0	1	n	
9	6	2	L⊗C∘R⊗L∘R⊗C∘T	0	1	y	
10	6	2	L⊗C∘L⊗R∘L⊗C∘T	2	2	n	
11	7	1	L∘R⊗L∘R⊗L∘R⊗C∘T	0	4	y	
12	7	2	L∘R⊗L∘C⊗R∘L⊗C∘T	1	1	n	St. Andrew
13	7	2	L∘R⊗C∘L⊗R∘L⊗C∘T	1	1	n	
14	7	2	L∘R⊗L∘C⊗L∘R⊗C∘T	1	2	y	
15	7	2	L∘R⊗C∘R⊗L∘R⊗C∘T	1	2	y	
16	7	2	L∘C⊗R∘L⊗R∘L⊗C∘T	1	2	n	
17	7	2	L∘C⊗L∘R⊗L∘R⊗C∘T	1	3	y	
18	7	3	L∘C⊗R∘C⊗L∘R⊗C∘T	0	1	y	Plattsburgh
19	7	3	L∘C⊗R∘C⊗R∘L⊗C∘T	0	2	n	
20	7	3	L∘C⊗L∘C⊗R∘L⊗C∘T	2	2	n	
21	7	3	L∘C⊗L∘C⊗L∘R⊗C∘T	2	3	y	
22	8	1	L⊗R∘L⊗R∘L⊗R∘L⊗C∘T	1	5	n	
23	8	2	L⊗R∘L⊗C∘R⊗L∘R⊗C∘T	0	2	y	Cavendish

24	8	2	L⊗R∘L⊗R∘C⊗L∘R⊗C∘T	0	2	y	
25	8	2	L⊗R∘C⊗L∘R⊗L∘R⊗C∘T	0	2	y	Christensen
26	8	2	L⊗R∘L⊗R∘C⊗R∘L⊗C∘T	0	3	n	
27	8	2	L⊗R∘C⊗R∘L⊗R∘L⊗C∘T	0	3	n	
28	8	2	L⊗C∘R⊗L∘R⊗L∘R⊗C∘T	0	3	y	
29	8	2	L⊗R∘L⊗C∘L⊗R∘L⊗C∘T	2	3	n	
30	8	2	L⊗C∘L⊗R∘L⊗R∘L⊗C∘T	2	4	n	
31	8	3	L⊗C∘R⊗L∘C⊗R∘L⊗C∘T	1	0	n	Windsor
32	8	3	L⊗C∘L⊗R∘C⊗L∘R⊗C∘T	1	1	y	
33	8	3	L⊗C∘R⊗L∘C⊗L∘R⊗C∘T	1	1	y	
34	8	3	L⊗R∘C⊗L∘C⊗R∘L⊗C∘T	1	1	n	
35	8	3	L⊗C∘L⊗R∘C⊗R∘L⊗C∘T	1	2	n	
36	8	3	L⊗R∘C⊗R∘C⊗L∘R⊗C∘T	1	2	y	
37	8	3	L⊗R∘C⊗L∘C⊗L∘R⊗C∘T	1	2	y	
38	8	3	L⊗C∘R⊗C∘L⊗R∘L⊗C∘T	1	2	n	
39	8	3	L⊗R∘C⊗R∘C⊗R∘L⊗C∘T	1	3	n	
40	8	3	L⊗C∘L⊗C∘R⊗L∘R⊗C∘T	1	3	y	
41	8	3	L⊗C∘R⊗C∘R⊗L∘R⊗C∘T	1	3	y	
42	8	3	L⊗C∘L⊗C∘L⊗R∘L⊗C∘T	3	4	n	
43	9	1	L∘R⊗L∘R⊗L∘R⊗L∘R⊗C∘T	0	6	y	
44	9	2	L∘R⊗L∘R⊗C∘L⊗R∘L⊗C∘T	1	3	n	Grantchester
45	9	2	L∘R⊗L∘C⊗R∘L⊗R∘L⊗C∘T	1	3	n	
46	9	2	L∘R⊗L∘R⊗L∘C⊗R∘L⊗C∘T	1	3	n	
47	9	2	L∘R⊗C∘L⊗R∘L⊗R∘L⊗C∘T	1	3	n	
48	9	2	L∘R⊗L∘R⊗C∘R⊗L∘R⊗C∘T	1	4	y	
49	9	2	L∘R⊗L∘C⊗L∘R⊗L∘R⊗C∘T	1	4	y	
50	9	2	L∘R⊗L∘R⊗L∘C⊗L∘R⊗C∘T	1	4	y	
51	9	2	L∘R⊗C∘R⊗L∘R⊗L∘R⊗C∘T	1	4	y	
52	9	2	L∘C⊗R∘L⊗R∘L⊗R∘L⊗C∘T	1	4	n	
53	9	2	L∘C⊗L∘R⊗L∘R⊗L∘R⊗C∘T	1	5	y	
54	9	3	L∘R⊗C∘L⊗R∘C⊗L∘R⊗C∘T	0	0	y	Hanover
55	9	3	L∘R⊗C∘R⊗L∘C⊗R∘L⊗C∘T	0	1	n	

56	9	3	L○R⊗C○L⊗R○C⊗R○L⊗C○T	0	1	n	
57	9	3	L○C⊗R○L⊗R○C⊗L○R⊗C○T	0	1	y	
58	9	3	L○C⊗R○L⊗C○R⊗L○R⊗C○T	0	1	y	
59	9	3	L○R⊗C○R⊗L○C⊗L○R⊗C○T	0	2	y	
60	9	3	L○C⊗R○L⊗R○C⊗R○L⊗C○T	0	2	n	
61	9	3	L○R⊗L○C⊗R○C⊗L○R⊗C○T	0	2	y	
62	9	3	L○R⊗C○L⊗C○R⊗L○R⊗C○T	0	2	y	
63	9	3	L○R⊗L○C⊗R○C⊗R○L⊗C○T	0	3	n	
64	9	3	L○R⊗C○R⊗C○L⊗R○L⊗C○T	0	3	n	
65	9	3	L○C⊗L○R⊗C○R⊗L○R⊗C○T	0	3	y	
66	9	3	L○C⊗R○C⊗L○R⊗L○R⊗C○T	0	3	y	
67	9	3	L○C⊗R○C⊗R○L⊗R○L⊗C○T	0	4	n	
68	9	3	L○C⊗L○R⊗L○C⊗R○L⊗C○T	2	2	n	
69	9	3	L○C⊗L○R⊗C○L⊗R○L⊗C○T	2	2	n	
70	9	3	L○C⊗R○L⊗C○L⊗R○L⊗C○T	2	2	n	
71	9	3	L○C⊗L○R⊗L○C⊗L○R⊗C○T	2	3	y	
72	9	3	L○R⊗L○C⊗L○C⊗R○L⊗C○T	2	3	n	
73	9	3	L○R⊗C○L⊗C○L⊗R○L⊗C○T	2	3	n	
74	9	3	L○R⊗L○C⊗L○C⊗L○R⊗C○T	2	4	y	
75	9	3	L○R⊗C○R⊗C○R⊗L○R⊗C○T	2	4	y	
76	9	3	L○C⊗L○C⊗R○L⊗R○L⊗C○T	2	4	n	
77	9	3	L○C⊗L○C⊗L○R⊗L○R⊗C○T	2	5	y	
78	9	4	L○C⊗R○C⊗L○C⊗R○L⊗C○T	1	2	n	Balthus
79	9	4	L○C⊗L○C⊗R○C⊗L○R⊗C○T	1	3	y	
80	9	4	L○C⊗R○C⊗R○C⊗L○R⊗C○T	1	3	y	
81	9	4	L○C⊗R○C⊗L○C⊗L○R⊗C○T	1	3	y	
82	9	4	L○C⊗L○C⊗R○C⊗R○L⊗C○T	1	4	n	
83	9	4	L○C⊗R○C⊗R○C⊗R○L⊗C○T	1	4	n	
84	9	4	L○C⊗L○C⊗L○C⊗R○L⊗C○T	3	4	n	
85	9	4	L○C⊗L○C⊗L○C⊗L○R⊗C○T	3	5	y	

APPENDIX

Tie Knots and Random Walks

Chapter 2 provided a qualitative summary of the theory of tie knots. This is how the theory appears to physicists.

Recall that in Chapter 2 we defined a tie knot as a sequence of moves chosen from the move set $\{R\odot, R\otimes, C\odot, C\otimes, L\odot, L\otimes\}$, initiated by $L\otimes$ or $L\odot$ and terminating with the subsequence $R\odot L\otimes C\odot T$ or $L\odot R\otimes C\odot T$. The sequence was constrained in such a way that no two consecutive moves indicate the same region or direction.

We now represent knot sequences as random walks on a triangular lattice. The axes r, c, l correspond to the three move regions R, C, L and the unit vectors $\hat{r}, \hat{c}, \hat{l}$ represent the corresponding moves (Figure A.1); we omit the directional notation $\odot, \otimes$ and the terminal action T. Since all knot sequences end with $C\odot$ and alternate between $\odot$ and $\otimes$, all knots of odd numbers of moves begin with $L\odot$ while those of even numbers of moves begin with $L\otimes$. Our simplified random walk notation is thus unique.

The three-fold symmetry of the move regions implies that only steps along the positive lattice axes are acceptable and, as in the case of moves, no consecutive steps can be identical. The latter condition makes our walk a second order Markov, or persistent, random walk. Nonetheless, every site on the lattice can be reached since, e.g., $-\hat{c} = \hat{r} + \hat{l}$ and $2\hat{c} = \hat{c} + \hat{l} + \hat{c} + \hat{r} + \hat{c}$.

The size of a knot, and the primary parameter by which we classify it, is the number of moves in the knot sequence, denoted by the half-winding number h. The initial and terminal sequence dictate that the smallest knot be given by the sequence $L\odot R\otimes C\odot T$, with $h = 3$. Practical (*viz.*, the finite length of the tie) as well as aesthetic considerations suggest an upper bound on knot size; we limit our exact results to half-winding number $h \leq 9$. The number of knots as a function of size, $K(h)$, corresponds to the number of walks of length h subject to the initial and terminal conditions.

We derive $K(h)$ by first considering all walks of length n beginning with $\hat{1}$, our initial constraint. Let $F_{\hat{r}}(n)$ be the number of walks beginning with $\hat{1}$ and ending with $\hat{r}$, $F_{\hat{c}}(n)$ the number beginning with $\hat{1}$ and ending with $\hat{c}$, etc. Accordingly, since at any given site the walker chooses between two steps,

$$F_{\hat{r}}(n) + F_{\hat{c}}(n) + F_{\hat{1}}(n) = 2^{n-1}. \tag{1}$$

Because the only permitted terminal sequences are $\hat{r}\,\hat{1}\,\hat{c}$ and $\hat{1}\,\hat{r}\,\hat{c}$, we are interested in the number of walks of length $n = h - 2$ ending with $\hat{r}$ or $\hat{1}$, after which the respective remaining two terminal steps may be concatenated.

We first consider $F_{\hat{1}}(n)$. Now $\hat{1}$ can only follow from $\hat{r}$ and $\hat{c}$ upon each additional step, that is,

$$F_{\hat{1}}(n + 2) = F_{\hat{r}}(n + 1) + F_{\hat{c}}(n + 1), \tag{2}$$

from which it follows that

$$F_{\hat{1}}(n + 2) = F_{\hat{r}}(n) + F_{\hat{c}}(n) + 2F_{\hat{1}}(n). \tag{3}$$

Combining (1) and (3) gives rise to the recursion relation

$$F_{\hat{1}}(n + 2) = F_{\hat{1}}(n) + 2^{n-1}, \tag{4}$$

with initial conditions $F_{\hat{1}}(1) = 1$ and $F_{\hat{1}}(2) = 0$.

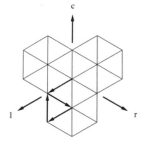

Figure A.1 *A tie knot may be represented by a persistent random walk on a triangular lattice, beginning with $\hat{1}$ and ending with $\hat{1}\,\hat{r}\,\hat{c}$ or $\hat{r}\,\hat{1}\,\hat{c}$. Only steps along the positive r, c and l axes are permitted and no two consecutive steps may be the same. Shown here is the four-in-hand, indicated by the walk $\hat{1}\,\hat{r}\,\hat{1}\,\hat{c}$.*

The recursion relation for $F_{\hat{r}}(n)$ is identical to (4), but with $F_{\hat{r}}(1) = 0$ and $F_{\hat{r}}(2) = 1$.

The number of knots of size h equals the number of walks of length $h - 2$ beginning with $\hat{l}$ and ending with $\hat{r}$ or $\hat{l}$. Accordingly,

$$K(h) = F_{\hat{r}}(h-2) + F_{\hat{l}}(h-2) = \tfrac{1}{3}\left(2^{h-2} - (-1)^{h-2}\right), \tag{5}$$

where $K(1) = K(2) = 0$, and the total number of knots is

$$\sum_{i=1}^{9} K(i) = 85. \tag{6}$$

The shape of a knot depends on the number of right, centre and left moves in the tie sequence. Since symmetry dictates an equal number of right and left moves (see below), knot shape is characterised by the number of centre moves γ. We use it to classify knots of equal size h; knots with identical h and γ belong to the same class. A large centre fraction $\frac{\gamma}{h}$ indicates a broad knot (e.g., the Windsor) and a small centre fraction suggests a narrow one (e.g., the four-in-hand). Some of the centre fractions of the 16 canonical knot classes, however, are sufficiently small not to admit aesthetic knots. We consequently limit our attention to $\frac{\gamma}{h} \in [\frac{1}{6}, \frac{1}{2}]$, where the lower bound is the centre fraction of the very narrow but occasionally worn Prince Albert knot. This leaves 13 aesthetic knot classes.

The number of knots in a class, $K(h, \gamma)$, corresponds to the number of walks of length h containing γ steps $\hat{c}$, beginning with $\hat{l}$ and ending with $\hat{r}\hat{l}\hat{c}$ or $\hat{l}\hat{r}\hat{c}$. The sequence of steps may be considered a coarser sequence of γ groups, each group composed of $\hat{r}$s and $\hat{l}$s and separated from other groups by a $\hat{c}$ on the right; the Windsor knot, for example, contains three groups, $\hat{l} \hat{c} \hat{r}\hat{l} \hat{c} \hat{r}\hat{l} \hat{c}$, of lengths 1, 2, 2, respectively. We refer to a particular assignment of the centre steps as a centre structure.

The number of centre structures is equivalent to the number of ordered ways of partitioning the integer $h - \gamma$ into γ positive integers,

$$P(h - \gamma, \gamma) = \binom{h - \gamma - 1}{\gamma - 1}, \tag{7}$$

subject to the terminal condition, which requires that the final group cannot be of length one. The latter condition reduces the possible centre structures by $\binom{h-\gamma-2}{\gamma-2}$.

The steps of each group may be ordered in two ways, beginning with $\hat{r}$ or beginning with $\hat{l}$, except for the first, which by assumption begins with $\hat{l}$. Accordingly, for a centre structure of γ groups, the number of walks is $2^{\gamma-1}$.

It follows that the number of knots in a class is

$$K(h, \gamma) = 2^{\gamma-1} \left(\binom{h-\gamma-1}{\gamma-1} - \binom{h-\gamma-2}{\gamma-2} \right) = 2^{\gamma-1} \binom{h-\gamma-2}{\gamma-1}. \tag{8}$$

The symmetry of a knot, which is our first aesthetic constraint, is defined as the absolute value of the number of moves to the right minus the number of moves to the left, i.e.,

$$s = \left| \sum_{i=1}^{h} x_i \right|, \tag{9}$$

where $x_i = 1$ if the ith step is $\hat{r}$, -1 if the ith step is $\hat{l}$ and 0 otherwise. We limit our attention to those knots from each class which minimise s.

Whereas the centre number γ and the symmetry s tell us the move composition of a knot, balance relates to the distribution of these moves; it corresponds to the extent to which the moves are well mixed. A well-balanced knot is tightly bound and keeps its shape. We use it as our second aesthetic constraint.

Let σ_i represent the ith step of the walk. The winding direction $\omega_i(\sigma_i, \sigma_i+1)$ is equal to 1 if the transition from σ_i to σ_i+1 is, say, clockwise and -1 otherwise. The balance b may then be expressed

$$b = \frac{1}{2} \sum_{i=2}^{h-1} \left| \omega_i - \omega_{i-1} \right|. \tag{10}$$

Of those knots which are maximally symmetric, the knot which minimises b is the most aesthetic of its class.

BIBLIOGRAPHY

Knots

Colin C. Adams, *The Knot Book: An Elementary Introduction to the Mathematical Theory of Knots* (Freeman and Co., New York, 1994).

Clifford W. Ashley, *The Ashley Book of Knots* (Faber and Faber, London, 1944). Reissued by Doubleday, New York, 1993.

Charles Livingston, *Knot Theory* (Mathematical Association of America, Washington, 1993).

Tie Knots

Anonymous, *Neckclothitania; or, Tietania* (J. J. Stockdale, London, 1818).

H. Le Blanc, *The Art of Tying the Cravat* (Effingham Wilson, London, 1828).

Thomas M. A. Fink and Yong Mao, 'Designing Tie Knots By Random Walks', *Nature*, vol. 398, p. 31 (1999).

Thomas M. A. Fink and Yong Mao, 'A Mathematical Theory of Tie Knots', *Physica A*, in press (1999).

Davide Mosconi and Riccardo Villarosa, *Getting Knotted* (Ratti, Milan, 1985). Republished as *The Book of Ties* (Tie Rack, London, 1985).

Ties

François Chaille, *The Book of Ties* (Flammarion, Paris, 1996).

Doriece Colle, *Collars, Stocks, Cravats* (Rodale Press, Emmaus, PA, 1972).

Roseann Ettinger, *20th Century Neckties* (Schiffer Publishing, Atglen, PA, 1998).

Sarah Gibbings, *The Tie* (Studio Editions, London, 1990).

Avril Hart, *Ties* (Victoria & Albert Museum, London, 1998).

A. Varron, 'Neckties', *Ciba Review*, vol. 38, p. 1361 (1941).

Men's Dress

Hardy Amies, *The Englishman's Suit* (Quartet, London, 1994).

A Cavalry Officer, *The Whole Art of Dress* (Effingham Wilson, London, 1830).

Farid Chenoune, *A History of Men's Fashion* (Flammarion, New York, 1993).

C. Willet Cunnington and Phillis Cunnington, *Handbook of English Costume in the 19th Century* (Faber and Faber, London, 1959).

Alan Flusser, *Style and the Man* (Villard, New York, 1988).

Clare Jerrold, *The Beaux and the Dandies* (Stanley Paul & Co., London, 1910).

James Laver, *Dandies* (Weidenfeld and Nicolson, London, 1968).

The 'Major' of To-Day, *Clothes and the Man* (Grant Richards, London, 1900).

Alan Mansfield and Phillis Cunnington, *Handbook of English Costume in the 20th Century, 1900–1950* (Faber and Faber, London, 1973).

Aileen Ribeiro and Valerie Cumming, *The Visual History of Costume* (Batsford, London, 1989).

O. E. Schoeffler and W. Gale, *Esquire's Encyclopedia of 20th Century Men's Fashion* (McGraw-Hill, New York, 1973).

The Duke of Windsor, *A Family Album* (Cassell, London, 1960).

INDEX

PICTURE CREDITS

AKG, London 15. BFI Stills Posters and Designs, London 132. Jean-Loup Charmet, Paris 20. Mary Evans Picture Library, London 16, 17, 25, 60. Ronald Grant Archive, London 65, 72, 76, 87, 95, 98, 104, 112. Hulton Getty Images/Central Press, London 119. National Gallery, London 12. National Portrait Gallery, London 34, 124. Private collections 21, 23, 27 (photo Bridgeman Art Library), 28, 35, 64, 78, 128 © Man Ray Trust/ADAGP, Paris and DACS, London 1999. *Punch* 1853, 42. Rex Features, London 69. Roger-Viollet, Paris 24, 32. Franklin D. Roosevelt Library, USA 84. University of Cambridge, Cavendish Laboratory endpapers, 31, 37. Vin Mag Archive, London 40.